Get **MORE** Customers For Your Business... *FAST!*

"Proven Marketing Systems That Quickly & Easily Make You More Money!"

****
Flip to Page 77 to Learn How to Claim Your FREE Custom Marketing Campaign
****

ANDREW JOHN COCKS

Watch This **FREE** Video Now & Discover A New Era Of Internet Marketing:
www.AndrewCocks.ca

Copyright, Limits of Liability/Disclaimer of Warranty:

Watch This **FREE** Video Now & Discover A New Era Of Internet Marketing:
www.AndrewCocks.ca

TABLE OF CONTENTS

CHAPTER 1   **Marketing Success Foundation:** Developing The Mindset To Achieve Massive Success In Your Business.. **11**

CHAPTER 2   **Successful Marketing Rules:** The New Rules About Marketing & Running Your Business In This Economy.. **33**

CHAPTER 3   **Customer Attraction Systems:** How To Stand Head And Shoulders Above Your Competitors While Attracting The Most Profitable Customers............ **53**

CHAPTER 4   **Million Dollar Marketing Messages:** Marketing Messages That Consistently Fill Your Business With High Quality Leads And Eager Prospects............ **61**

CHAPTER 5   **Online Marketing Systems:** Using The Power Of The Internet To Increase Your Sales And Profits.. **69**

CHAPTER 6   **Loyalty Marketing Systems:** How To Practically Guarantee That Your Customers Buy From You For Life!... **81**

CHAPTER 7   **Referral Marketing Systems:** How To Generate Massive Sales And Profits By Getting Referrals From Your Customers & Local Businesses................ **93**

CHAPTER 8   **Follow-Up Marketing Systems:** How To Consistently Generate Massive Amounts of Leads, Sales And Profits From Your In-House Database. **103**

CHAPTER 9   **Profit Maximization Systems:** How To Consistently Generate More Sales And Profits Without Spending More Money On Advertising......................... **119**

Watch This **FREE** Video Now & Discover A New Era Of Internet Marketing:
www.AndrewCocks.ca

PREFACE

If you have been sitting on the fence trying to figure out how you can leverage marketing tools like Funnels, Websites, Autoresponders, Facebook, Twitter, YouTube and Smartphones to get more leads into your business, then the fact that massive success in your business is closer now than it's ever been, should have you salivating with excitement.

In fact, the current state of the economy that we find ourselves in is the perfect storm for business owners who are nimble and willing to ride the wave. However, taking advantage of this new economy comes with one requirement: You must take action *now*.

No more stalling, no more procrastination, no more day-dreaming about what it will feel like once you have a business that runs smoothly and successfully without you. No longer can you straddle the fence, waiting and hoping that an ad rep strolls through your doors and magically solves all your marketing problems. See, the truth is that you are guaranteed to continue struggling if you are sitting back and hoping that you can buy the magic bullet.

What you hold in your hands is the ultimate step-by-step blueprint to take you by the hand and guide you through the danger-riddled, but rewarding journey of setting up marketing systems that will get customers into your business *today*.

In this book, I have compiled dozens of marketing strategies that successful business owners are using right now to consistently break sales and revenue records month after month. None of these strategies are untested theoretical ideas that haven't seen the light of day. Each marketing strategy and system has been painstakingly applied and leveraged to produce tens of thousands of dollars in profits each and every week in every type of business imaginable.

I have included the information you will want to have to know in order to effectively market your business, but more importantly, I have included the information that you will NEED to know to avoid getting ripped off, losing your sanity or giving up on your dream.

The book you hold in your hands is unique in four major ways:

1. This book…is meant to be used as your personal guide to marketing your business. There are plenty of books about running a business, but this is the one of the most comprehensive books to extensively focus on marketing your business in today's economy.

2. This book…prepares you to become an expert at getting leads into your business by empowering you with the exact information you need to know to market your business. Nothing has been left out.

3. This book…breaks down all the vital parts of writing marketing messages that gets butts into your business. It is not just a few scattered pages about marketing online, ads, training staff and so on. This book gives you the birds-eye view and then swoops down for an in-the-trenches inspection of each piece of the marketing formula.

4. This book…hands you the keys to unlock every piece of knowledge and resource that you will need to successfully market your business.

~ 8 ~

After reading this one-of-a-kind business marketing blueprint you will know:

1. How to use a simple piece of paper and a pencil to create marketing pieces that bring in thousands of dollars to your business within five to ten days.

2. The easy way to setup marketing systems that run on autopilot and allow you to increase your profits by more than you've ever dreamed would be possible.

3. The security of success because you'll finally be confident in yourself because you have the knowledge, tools and resources to stabilize your sales, profits and personal income.

By investing in this book, you opened the door to an entire library of information about marketing your business that will serve as guiding lights of inspiration, encouragement and sometimes an occasional slap on the wrist ;)

See you at the top,

ANDREW JOHN COCKS

CHAPTER 1

Marketing Success Foundation: Developing The Mindset To Achieve Massive Success In Your Business

The first chapter is called marketing success foundation and this chapter is all about developing the mindset to achieve massive success in your business. In this chapter, you'll discover why just focusing on trying to cover payroll and make a little extra is killing your business. By the end of this chapter, you will know how to use your competitors to catapult your business to a whole new level and attract your ideal customers.

This chapter will also help you overcome your doubts and self-destructive habits that are holding you back in your personal life and your business success. I will also reveal the real secret behind the success of millionaire business owners and teach you how to leverage their success and use it to achieve what you want to achieve in your own business. Lastly, we'll talk about the eight key areas in your business that you must measure and track on a daily basis in order to know how well your marketing efforts are working for your business.

~ 11 ~

However, the fact of the matter is that in order for you to have any level of success with the strategies discussed in this book, you have to first embrace the same mindset, beliefs, habits and goals of other successful business owners. The harsh reality is…without the right mindset, beliefs, habits and goals, unfortunately, you're destined to fail. There is no magic pill and nothing I can teach you here that will overcome poor habits, lack of discipline and self-doubt.

If you're serious about your success, then your real foundation, the true starting point for you is that you have to address what's going on between your ears– what your belief, what your mindset is, what your habits are and what your goals are.

Tested And Proven to Work

The strategies and systems in this book work and they're not classroom theory or untested ideas. These strategies form the foundation for thousands of successful business owners right now, all over the country. The only thing that will stop them from working for you is your own mindset. That's why you need to first address what's going on between your own two ears.

Within the pages of this book, everything you thought you knew about marketing your business will be challenged, pushed and pulled in different directions by the strategies and concepts in this book. Trust me when I tell that's a good thing because at the end of this book, you will finally have a blueprint for marketing success in your business and that's what matters.

How Bad Do You Want It?

Let me ask you this: How bad do you really want it? Are you tired of struggling? Are you tired of the empty days and your staff standing around in your business with nothing to do for hours at a time?

In order to get the most out of this book, you have to look within yourself and answer the question of how bad do you really want real success in your business. There will also be things in this book that will challenge your closely held beliefs. That's intentional, but at the end of the day…it doesn't matter what your employees think. It doesn't matter what your "mother-in-law" thinks. It doesn't matter what the guy down the street thinks. It doesn't matter that you'll never win a most beautiful advertising award for your marketing pieces. It doesn't even matter if it strokes your ego or not.

All that really matters is that the strategies in this book will put money in your bank account and help your business become more successful. That's what this entire book is about.

My definition of a successful business is a business that consistently generates a profit that pays you a very nice salary of your own choosing. It's a business that creates a financially valuable asset that allows you to live the lifestyle that you choose to live and doesn't require you to work like a dog for it to operate successfully.

That's my definition of a successful business. Hopefully, that's what your definition sounds like too.

Now, here's what success is not: working yourself into an early grave because you're trapped in a business for eighteen or more hours a day. It is not success if you are terrified to pick up the phone when it rings because it might be a bill collector. It is not success when you are going through multiple divorces because you're a nervous wreck and a stressed out jerk, or missing out on seeing your kids grow up because you're stuck at the business for weeks at a time.

That is not success by any stretch of anyone's imagination. But that is exactly what many business owners experience. The reason for many of their struggles is due to the fact that they have not learned how to successfully market and operate their business.

Let's be honest. Nobody buys a business with the intention of working 90+ hours a week, getting paid less than minimum wage, having their reputation publicly trashed by complete strangers while risking going broke every few months and facing a life of bitter poverty.

Nobody buys or opens a business with that in mind. But that is essentially what has happened thousands of times all over the country to business owners.

See, it's one thing to say that you want real success in your business, but it's an entirely different thing to actually make that success a reality. So, I'm going to give it to you straight and you'll never again wonder how the other guys are doing it. You'll know exactly how they're doing it.

Your True Business Success Foundation

There are five major ingredients that you need to have in order to turn your business around and become truly successful:

1. You must **think** like a successful business owner
2. You must **believe** you can actually be a successful business owner
3. You must **set goals** like a successful business owner.
4. You must **model** the systems of a successful business owner.
5. You must **measure and track** key performance indicators like a successful business owner would do.

Ingredient #1 – What You Think

Every breakthrough and success you'll have in your business starts with a simple thought in your mind. Thoughts are the seeds that grow into sales, profits and revenues.

If you can change the way you think, you can change your entire life and your business. But you need to guard your mind like your life depends on it because in fact your life does depend on your mind. You can't be passive about what you're reading, watching and listening to. You must be a vigilant soldier of your mindset.

Successful Business Owner Difference #1

Successful business owners think about all the ways they can charge higher prices for a premium experience. Successful business owners constantly brainstorm ways that they can offer premium experiences and products and value so that they feel justified in charging premium prices.

So, instead of competing on price, their focus is on quality; quality products and quality services at a premium price. By the way, yes they are sensitive to their customers' desire for a good deal and value, but they know that people choose businesses, services and products for many other reasons besides the price.

They realize that no matter how little they charge, someone can always charge less, so successful business owners don't play the lowest price game and neither should you.

Successful Business Owner Difference #2

Successful business owners think about the habits they need to develop in order to accomplish their big goals. The truth of the matter is that your habits will either serve as a springboard to your next level of your success or serve as a quicksand pit that keeps you stuck at current level or brings you even further down.

These successful habits include things like:

- ➢ Attending business marketing and management conferences on a regular basis.
- ➢ Investing in and reading books and business improvement books on a regular basis.
- ➢ Weekly meeting with staff and employees to track and review goals.
- ➢ Managing inventory and payment processing with an online system point of sale.

Successful Business Owner Difference #3

Successful business owners read, watch and listen to things that support their belief that success is truly possible in every area of their business. It's a proven fact that if you truly believe something is possible, you tend to focus on the ways to make that possibility a reality.

Also, if you don't think something is possible, then you will tend to focus on why it can't be done. There are three stages of possibility thinking that people can either get stuck in or go through:

1. Thinking nothing is possible no matter what they do.
2. Thinking that something is possible.
3. Thinking that anything is possible.

So, here's the question you need to ask yourself...

"When presented with a challenge, do I first think of the ways you could succeed or the ways I could fail?"

High achieving business owners are always looking for ways to get to the level of success that they envision in their mind.

The only real question for successful business owners is what they must change or do to get to the next level of success and is that how you view your business?

Successful Business Owner Difference #4

Successful business owners know that they'll never be successful if they're always stuck doing grunt work. The top business owners have a very specific view of their role as the owner and what they should and should not be doing in their businesses.

They spend their time developing new marketing campaigns, creating new lines of business and adapting to constantly changing local market conditions. They know the value of creating systems for interviewing, selecting and hiring new employees, managing staff and using standard processes and procedures for every area of their business.

Successful Business Owner Difference #5

Successful business owners are able to move forward with good plans and marketing strategies even if they are afraid. One of the big obstacles for most business owners is that they take one or more steps forward, but because they hit a few roadblocks or issues, they then become paralyzed by the fear of failing.

When most business owners feel that fear, they tend to give in and lose all the momentum they've gained instead of stopping and reflecting on what's truly going on in their heart and mind which is what successful business owners do.

In some cases, successful business owners are able to even use the fear of failure to motivate themselves to take massive action instead of being frozen with fear.

Successful Business Owner Difference #6

Successful business owners know that they have to try many ideas and tactics to get the results they desire. See, if you know the odds of you succeeding are ten to one. Then, you also know that if you have ten attempts, you're practically guaranteed to succeed at least once. All you need is ten attempts to guarantee your success.

Successful business owners are able to control and manage their perception of the journey that they're taking on the road to their success. It doesn't matter if you think that the glass is half full or the glass is half empty…both are right. It just boils down to your perspective on this situation.

Successful business owners know that failure is just stepping-stones on their journey to success. They experience temporary setbacks and then build upon it to prevent it from happening again. Then, they move forward again from there.

Successful Business Owner Difference #7

Successful business owners know that they can quickly grow their business to huge levels of profits by finding creative ways to co-partner with other businesses. There are dozens of groups, business organizations and companies that would love to partner with you.

When you become the "business of choice" for several local businesses, you gain access to thousands of customers that you don't have to pay advertising costs to get. Yes, it might mean donating products and services at events occasionally, but the extra profits you generate will more than make up for that expense.

Because at the end of the day, you can add thousands of prospects to your marketing lists and databases without paying thousands of dollars of marketing expenses.

Successful Business Owner Difference #8

Successful business owners create and maintain standards for themselves and their employees so that they can consistently deliver excellence as their business grows in size. The key is to clearly define what performance standards you need and then holding everyone accountable to meeting or exceeding those levels.
The standards that successful business owners develop and implement are then used as part of their advertising and marketing

campaign to help them stand head and shoulders above their competitors. Developing and implementing high standards in your business sets you on the path for tremendous success as your business grows.

Successful Business Owner Difference #9

Successful business owners deliver an almost unbelievably high level of service that can rarely be matched. Successful business owners have a burning desire to serve their customers. They always focus on delivering a high level of service.

These business owners know exactly why people should choose their business and are able to tell their prospects in clear terms. They rarely argue with a customer over an incorrect or mistaken order. The successful business owner knows what's really at stake in that transaction.

The successful business owner is always testing new products, services, vendors and combinations of all of them in order to continuously raise the standard of service in their business.

Successful Business Owner Difference #10

Successful business owners embrace new technology and cutting-edge marketing strategies. If you're still depending on fliers, door hangers and television commercials, then you're likely a few months away from bankruptcy.

Successful business owners know that text message marketing, online marketing strategies and current marketing strategies bring hundreds of customers each month like clockwork. That's y you have to keep an open mind you have to keep an open mind to any marketing strategy that can be applied successfully to your business.

And yes, you must include proven traditional strategies, I'm not saying you throw those out of the window. But you **MUST** layer new cutting edge strategies on top of that foundation.

Ingredient #2 – What You Believe

Your belief system goes hand-in-hand with your success mindset. They are inseparable. Many business owners have been one strategy or tweak away from success, but they stopped believing so they never experienced the level of success they wanted.

Without your belief, the seed you've planted in your heart and mind will wither and die. If you don't believe, then it's no surprise that your employees, spouse and customers also don't believe.

Successful Business Owner Belief #1:

"A marketing strategy can only be successful if I fully implement it and test it out for an extended amount of time."

No matter how great and awesome a marketing strategy is, the marketing strategy is only as good as the business owner who is implementing it.

You've got to implement the entire strategy before you can see if it works for you. You have no chance of it working if you don't even try it.

Once you get a strategy implemented, you have to let it run for at least 90 days so you can see the results and change things to get better results. You should always start by testing any strategy you're thinking of doing on a small part of your customers and if that works, roll it out to all your customers.

Successful Business Owner Belief #2:

"If there is a marketing strategy that works in other businesses, then it can work in my business and in my market too"

While you may need to tweak or adjust the specifics of the marketing strategy, if it has been done in another business in another market, it can be done in your market.

When a business owner says "It can't be done in my market" what that means is that they are saying they haven't found the right way to make it work in their business" and until they actually try an approach that worked in another business, you will never know whether it can or can't be done in yours.

Successful Business Owner Belief #3:

"It's always better to invest a week or two initially setting up a process, system or strategy so that I can profit from that work for many years to come."

Successful business owners are true believers in doing the hard work once and benefiting from that hard work over and over again. Here's how it can go you can continue to work 110+ hours a week and make $60,000 a year or you can put in 20 hours of work once and earn a high six figure income every year for the rest of your life.

Understanding that your income will not necessarily increase because you work more hours is always a tough concept for most business owners to accept, but it's true. You have to get into the habit of focusing really intensely for short periods of time to get strategies and systems implemented and then you can just spend a couple of hours a week optimizing and tracking the results and making changes based on the feedback.

Successful Business Owner Belief #4:

"As long as a marketing strategy generates customers, sales and profits, then it's not too expensive."

You're an entrepreneur, so by default you're putting it all on the line which means you will always have a certain level of risk no matter what you do. Therefore, a marketing strategy is only too expensive if it doesn't return an acceptable profit. Managing the risk of investing money in marketing for your business can be easily managed by investing small amounts on a scheduled basis and then tracking your results before investing more.

Any dollar you spend that increases your net profits is ultimately a dollar well invested. It's not too risky when you break your marketing investment down into smaller dollar amounts and track your results to see what's working.

Successful Business Owner Belief #5:

"Having good products & services, a great location and trained staff are no longer good enough by themselves. I need to carve out a special place in the hearts and minds of my customers."

In this new economy, the old business success formula is no longer good enough to succeed. Yes, you still need good products, yes you need good service and yes you still need a competent staff, but in this day and age of competition, you also need to focus on selling a unique experience.

To reach your highest level of success with your business, you must have a consistent and enjoyable experience for your customers every time they visit your business. Then, you must ensure that your staff consistently delivers that experience according to the systems and standards you've set in place.

Successful Business Owner Belief #6:

~ 22 ~

"I must invest in attending conferences, books and hiring qualified experts to help me always improve my business."

You should make it a habit to attend at least one industry conference and one marketing conference a year. There you will find business owners who have been in your exact situation and have figured out great solutions to the exact problem you're facing. They'll happily share their knowledge with you.

You also have to make it your personal mission to buy up books and training books by industry experts so that you stay ahead of your competitors. Once you've uncovered a problem that you can't solve or if you want to reach your goals faster, then it's time to bring in the experts.

Successful Business Owner Belief #7:

"The amount of sales and profits that I make are directly dependent on my ability to train, lead, inspire and manage my staff."

Obviously you can't run an entire business by yourself, so it's vital that you build strong teams of loyal, dedicated and committed staff that will carry out your vision. If you spend all of your time doing everything personally, then you'll never be able to reach the higher levels that you want.

Your staff must know their daily, weekly and monthly goals and be properly trained, supported and managed in order to reach those goals. You must have your systems and processes down to an exact science so that all team members know their goals and responsibilities and goals.

Ingredient #3 – Your Goals

Now that you have set your mind, clarified your thinking, and strengthened your beliefs, it's time to know and set your goals. Here's how a successful business owner **sets goals** for their business that's different from average business owners.

In order to set goals, you need to answer one question. This will serve as your leading point towards a successful business… and that question is very simple…

Where Are You Headed?

Many business owners float aimlessly from one cash crisis to the next cash crisis. That's a terrible way to run your business and it's an even worse way to live. At a minimum, you need to have daily, weekly and monthly goals. The smaller goals that you set will serve as your road map to your bigger goals. You see, knowing where you're headed will set yourself to the right direction so achieving big goals should be tightly guided by your smaller daily, weekly, and monthly goals.

Do You Have Big Goals For Your Business?

Tiny goals equal tiny results. Here are some examples of tiny goals:
You settle for your business just being half-full on Thursday, Friday and Saturday evenings. Or sometimes, you are just trying to cover your overhead expenses and having a little bit left over. Then, you take most of that little bit that's left over and use it to try and prove to your spouse see that things are okay. Another tiny goal is keeping a fishbowl around your business to collect a few business cards.

Those are small tiny goals, and they give you tiny results. Now, here are some big goals that get you big results. First, you consistently fill your business every day of the week. Then you attract 100-300 brand new first-time customers each week. You pack out your business at lunch and dinner time every single day of the week and get featured in your local newspapers and media regularly. Best of all, you are having customers call and reserve tables for any day of the week that you can fit them in and then finally expanding your business through franchising or opening up different locations.

Aren't those great goals and great results? Honestly, which one sounds more like you? See, the fact is..."

"You will become as small as your controlling desire; or as great as your dominant aspiration."

So, you become as small as your thinking, or as great as your big goals. So don't be afraid to chase greatness.

The truth is that most great achievements in life are the result of thinking big and aiming high. Small goals put chains, restrictions and limits on your potential, but when you're working towards a big goal you barrel right through tons of smaller goals by virtue of chasing the big goal. However, in order to become your very best is to think at a very high level.

Chasing Greatness

The truth is that most great achievements in life are the result of thinking big and aiming high. Small goals they put chains, restrictions and limits on your potential, but when you're working towards a big goal you barrel right through tons of smaller goals by virtue of chasing that big goal. However in order to become your very best you have to think at a very high level in regards to your goals.

Ingredient #4 – Modeling Success

Modeling the proven systems and processes of other successful businesses is the missing ingredient that most business owners are looking for. Imagine having the exact strategies, process and systems that other successful business owners have used to explode their profits.

ways to get more customers. It's all there waiting for you they've done the work for you. However, the profits are not in simply having the blueprint in your hand but the real gold the real profit the real breakthrough lies in your ability to actually implement the strategies you don't need to re-invent the wheel.

Don't Reinvent The Wheel!!

Don't fall for the classic mistake of thinking that you are the only one who doesn't have enough money for advertising or that you're the only one being crowded out by big chain stores and things like that.

Every problem or challenge you have in your business has already been faced and solved by other successful business owners. You just have to put their solution into action in your business. The real issue will be in finding the solution, but since you've invested in this book, you already have many of the answers you have been looking for.

The Power of Modeling

You have to start using blueprints or roadmaps by other successful business owners and it will dramatically decrease the amount of time and money you waste. That's why it's so important that you attend conferences, events and invest in resources by other successful business owners.

In regards to the power of modeling others success, Tony Robbins wrote in his book titled Unlimited Power:

- Long ago, he realized that success leaves clues, that people who produce outstanding results do specific things to create those results.
- Modeling is the pathway to excellence. . . .The movers and shakers of the world are often professional modelers—

people who have mastered the art of learning everything they can by following other people's experience rather than just relying on their own.

- To model excellence you should be a detective, an investigator, someone who asks lots of questions and tracks down all the clues to what produces that excellence. . Building from the successes of others is one of the fundamental aspects of most learning

But, even when you find successful business systems and process to model, you will have to overcome the final hurdle.

The Hidden Pitfall of Modeling

The irony is that when most struggling business owners get to peek behind the curtain of successful businesses, they're quickly bored and unimpressed with the proven systems and processes that million dollar businesses are using.

They often complain that it seems too simple and easy. They can't get their heads around how simple it can be to achieve massive success in their business. So, they go back to their businesses and either never attempt the strategy or make it so complicated that they give up on it.

The Hidden Path To Success?

Most business owners incorrectly think that the road to success is hidden away, and if you could find it, it would be twisting, uphill, covered in fog, and full of pitfalls. Therefore many struggling business owners:

- Distrust obvious and straight forward answers to their problems

- They Complicate simple concepts because we think the truth is too "common sense."
- And they tend to gravitate towards the secretive and mysterious because they believe that they hold magical alluring qualities.

Model Your Way to Success

Successful business owners know that their success is dependent on their ability to discover the simple but powerful things that they can consistently do to grow their business. They know that the more complicated it is, the less likely their staff will be able to implement it consistently.

No matter how simple it looks, they do it and test the results and you need to do the same for yourself. After all, a small round wheel is not complicated but yet it revolutionized the world.

Ingredient #5 – Measure & Tracking

It's a well-known fact among successful business owner's that you can't improve what you don't measure or track. In successful business's knowing the daily, weekly and monthly numbers is as common as putting on shoes. They wouldn't dare dream of drifting aimlessly from day to day without knowing their numbers.

However, struggling business owners do exactly that. You must know all the important numbers in your business in order to make the right decisions that lead to lasting profits.

Key Area #1: Attracting New Customers

Customers are the lifeblood of your business. Without a consistent flow of LOYAL customers, your business is slowly but surely going out of business. You should have several marketing campaigns that are always bringing new customers to your business.

It's important that you're tracking your numbers in your business. At the most basic level, you should know the following two numbers:

- How many new leads you get each day.
- How many new customers you get each day.
- What ad or marketing message brought the lead in and turned them into customers.

Key Area #2: Track Lead Sources

This seems obvious, but many business owners don't track how many of their customers are coming in from their various marketing efforts. If you don't know what's working, then you may be wasting a ton of money on things that don't work.

You should know exactly what marketing strategies are working to bring people through your doors. The best way to do this is by providing a tracking system that could consist of a coupon, unique code or phrase that a customer must bring with them in order to get the deal advertised on the marketing piece.

Key Area #3: Lifetime Value of Customers

Successful business owners know the lifetime value of each customer that walks into their business. This is important because it determines how much you can invest on marketing and advertising to get and keep your customers.

So, if on average a customer comes to your business twice a month for an average of five years and spends on average $20 per visit, then their lifetime value is $2,400. Keep in mind that we're talking averages here, so that means that on average every one of your customers is worth $2,400 to you over five years. Therefore, is it reasonable to invest $3 per customer to get them to come back to your business again and again? Heck yeah it is!

Key Area #4: Staff

It is virtually impossible to maximize your business's sales potential without your staff performing at their best. Your staff training is just as important as any other part of your business.

Here are the three main areas that you need to train on:

1. Recruiting - What kind of people do I have?
2. Training -What training needs do I have?
3. Management -What performance or accountability issues do I have?

Key Area #5: Technology & Tools

It will be next to impossible for you to succeed in this new economy if you are not embracing current technology and tools. However, the technology you use in your business must always help you reach real tangible goals. Technology tools can include everything from computers, software, and marketing systems.

The questions you must ask yourself are:

1. What new systems or tools do you need to add?
2. What current systems or tools do you need to improve or upgrade?

Key Area #6: Personal Education & Growth

Your personal education should be prioritized and invested in just like any other part of your business. There are new marketing strategies and new technologies that can make a tremendous impact on the success of your business, but you must stay current on the knowledge.

Without your own personal development, you won't have the skills and knowledge to sustain the growth in your business. You need to ask yourself the following questions:

1. What knowledge do I need to learn?
2. What skills do I need to acquire?

If you're currently not measuring or tracking any of the key performance indicators I just covered, then it will seem overwhelming when you finally start. But, do it anyway. It's not about what's easy, but it's about what works.

Start with simple tracking sheets that are included in this book and add your own custom performance indicators to those. The sooner you start tracking, the sooner you can improve.

Watch This **<u>FREE</u>** Video Now & Discover A New Era Of Internet Marketing:
www.AndrewCocks.ca

CHAPTER 2

New Age Marketing: The New Rules About Marketing Your Business In This Economy

Unless you've been living under a rock, you've noticed that the economy has changed and that attracting more leads and customers and keeping your existing customers happy is harder than ever before.

Have You Noticed?

Have you noticed that ads and promotions that worked in the good ole' days, don't do diddly-squat now? Or that they don't do much now and that they don't get many customers in now? Have you also noticed how it's costing you more and more just to break even and you feel lucky for even doing just that? Have you noticed that new businesses are opening up all around your place and you're losing customers left and right? Have you even realized that people that used to come in two to three times a week are now coming in once or twice a month? Have you tried going into other businesses and noticed that they are copying you and lowering their prices and are pulling your long-term loyal customers away from you? Have you also noticed that things like coupon books just aren't working anymore?

Long story short, it's tough out here right now, but why is it so much harder now to get more customers for your business than it was before? Well, it's because you're probably violating one or more of the new rules of running and marketing your business in this new economy! And then now you're asking, "What exactly are the new rules?"

New Rule #1 of Business Marketing

The customer has the only vote that counts. Period.

One of the biggest marketing mistakes business owners make is not understanding and addressing customer needs. Most business owners NEVER ask their customers for feedback about what they did or didn't like about their business.

The biggest breakthroughs in your business usually come from your customers, but you must get the information from them. Including but not limited to: knowing what motivates the customers to choose your business over your competitors. You also have to know what's most important to them when choosing a business. Or you may ask yourself, *"Do they want the lowest price or the best product or service for a premium price?"*

You have to know these kinds of things in order to understand your customers or clients and to let them know that they have an important role to play in your business.

New Rule #2 of Business Marketing

You must test everything in your business first in order to improve upon it. Instead of guessing, test it out in an ad or on a customer and get their feedback.

Don't underestimate how powerful this is. You must test every component of your marketing pieces. If they don't at least pay for themselves, stop doing it. The only way to test something is to require the prospect to take a specific action upon seeing the advertisement.

This is called direct response advertising or direct response marketing. It allows you to measure and track the effectiveness of all your marketing. It requires the prospect or the customer in this case to bring a coupon or some kind of tracking mechanism into your business so that you know what advertisement or marketing message brought them into your business.

New Rule #3 of Business Marketing

Prospects need a unique, persuasive and compelling reason to choose your business over your competitors.
Every customer always wants to know what's in it for them. Don't waste your time with the normal self-promotional and bragging image advertising. Nobody cares how many awards and things like that you've got in the past. They want a good meal, they want a good experience and they want it at a good price.

Your marketing message must be specific to your prospects needs, wants and problems. You need a unique selling proposition (USP) that tells people exactly why they should choose your business over any and every available option to them, including eating at home.

New Rule #4 of Business Marketing

Stop trying to attract anyone and everyone to your business. You should only focus on attracting the best type of customer to your business.

You must pick a specific type of customer that you want to target and then tailor a specific marketing campaign to that specific type of customer. In your business marketing campaign, you should never try to list everything you offer. Pick one.

In your business marketing campaign, you should never try to list everything you offer. Pick one thing and focus on it at a time. Not everyone will appreciate your products and services. That's a fact of life. Your ads need to be specific and compelling to draw a specific type of customer.

This is usually a tough one for your business because most business owners would want to believe that everyone should like their food or everyone should like their business but that's just not the case.

New Rule #5 of Business Marketing

Customers must enjoy both the products, services and experience of buying from your business. Get one of these wrong and you're guaranteed to struggle.

Make sure you're staff isn't slow to offer help or being rude to customers, because if so, customers won't stick around to give you another shot there are just too many options out there.

Don't compromise on quality and variety to lower the cost. If anything, have separate lines of products to meet the needs of every type of customer. Also, don't ever compromise on giving the best customer service but you should always strive to give the best shopping experience for your customers at all times.

Finally, make it your mission to continually ask your customers about what they would recommend you do in order to improve your business.

New Rule #6 of Business Marketing

You must take scheduled time away from your business to improve and implement the things that are important to your customers.

In order for you to view your business from your customer's or customer's perspective, you must take time to step away from your business and look at it from a customer's perspective.

Bear in mind that your business is not your life. Your business and your life are completely separate things. The key is to step outside your own shoes and begin to come up with new and exciting ways to get more customers and get your current customers to continue to come back.

Scheduled time to improve and implement—this is the highlight of this new rule. You can choose to do it every 6 months or once every quarter, or you may take a day or two to look at your numbers, revenues, sales, inventory, and all the different things that you needed to look at. This will help you figure out the area where you are weak.

You need to discover all the things that are going to keep your business successful and all the things that keep the balance in your life. And to do that, you need to take a scheduled time away from your business at least once every six months or once every quarter.

New Rule #7 of Business Marketing

You can't do everything all by yourself, because it dramatically limits what you're able to accomplish.

If it's only you, then when you run out of time, money, energy, ideas, etc., there's going to be nothing and nobody else to help you.

Many business owners think that they can do things by themselves if only they work harder. I say, don't fall into the trap of working harder, but getting less and less results. For example, do you earn twice as much if you work twice harder? No.

This is where the role of your staff comes. Your staff is very essential for your business. You must get your staff properly trained and implement technology where it's appropriate to help you make dramatic increases towards your goals and results.

New Rule #8 of Business Marketing

Stop reinventing the wheel every single time because of a lack of effective systems.

If your business is not built on proven systems that you can easily teach your staff, then all you really have is a job that requires you to start over from the beginning every single day. This means that you need a system for everything—a system for attracting new customers, for collecting their contact information and providing them with superior service, for turning customers into lifetime customers and then getting them to refer others to your business.

You need systems for all of these things because the thing about a system that's so great—the reason why you need it in your business—is because you need to know that you need to approach your marketing systems the same way you approach your serving systems. You need to have these marketing systems in place to collect information and to keep people coming to your business because nothing happens until somebody buys something.

New Rule #9 of Business Marketing

You must actively get reviews and testimonials from your customers. And how do you do this in this new economy?

We live in an age of social media where everyone is connected and very vocal about the businesses they love or hate. You can't simply sit around and hope that people say good things about your business. You need to be proactive and get customers to open up about the things they liked and then document it so you can use it on your website and in your marketing.

Accomplish this by having your staff hand out comment feedback cards with every purchase and give them a little script to say as well.

The whole point of this is that you want your staff to prompt your customers to write down their feedback. You may want to invest on hand held cameras where they can get the customer on camera and tell them to say something positive about their visit.

Do this and you'll see that over time, say 30 to 60-day time period, you could easily get a hundred to two hundred testimonials that you could use on your website. You could use them in your marketing. You could get these people to go to Yelp or any number of review websites and leave their comments and feedbacks which in turn get you more customers and get more people to come to your business.

New Rule #10 of Business Marketing

You must list your business in every online business directory and review website that your customers use online to find businesses like yours.

The large majority of people have a tablet or smart phone that they use to search for everything under the sun.

You or your staff should be handing out feedback cards that encourage and rewards customers for posting a review on specific social media websites and review websites. Be sure to ask the customers to email a link to their review on the specific website so that you can use it in your marketing.

The best way to get these reviews and testimonials is to reward your customers with a benefit, bonus or freebie. It works wonders. This has to become a regular practice in your business.

New Rule #11 of Business Marketing

Build your in-house database by collecting the contact details, birthday and anniversary date (if applicable) of every customer.

The biggest mistake that most business owners make is to not collect the contact information of their customers.

You should have two or three ways to capture a customer's contact information at every visit to your business. For example you can offer to sign them up for your discount club, V.I.P. customers club or even offer them a free giveaway.

You should make it a weekly or monthly contest among your staff to see who can collect the most contact capture forms or you can pay a certain amount per contact form.

Why Build A Database?

The best part about building your own in-house database is that you can generate profits at any time by offering the contacts in your database a new enticing offer or special pricing to boost your sales and revenues. This means that you can get off the sales revenue roller coaster and control the sales flow in your business.

Also, your business will no longer be held hostage by the high costs of traditional marketing strategies and plus you can test out new ideas and strategies without having to spend thousands of dollars to get new customers.

Missed Opportunity…

Most business owners spend thousands of dollars trying to get the attention of a small percentage of people who may possibly come to their business, but do little to keep in contact with people who have already shopped and purchased from their business.

Business Insurance

Building a list of past customers that you can market your business to on-demand is your insurance policy against the revenue roller coaster most business owners have to endure.

Your database should be filled with hundreds of past customers who you can email and send your promotional offers to any time you want.

Imagine the power of sending out an email, text message, postcard or letter on Tuesday and having a waiting list for the next two weeks from that one marketing effort. That's powerful. That's what having an in-house list of past customers can do for you.

So Don't Be An Average Joe

Don't be an average business owner. Don't spend thousands of dollars on advertising with newspaper, radio, television, postcards or letters then wish and hope the ad is good enough to attract new customers to cover the costs of ad and make a little profit only to end with them coming to your business but never hearing from you again. That's a tragedy that's replayed over and over in businesses all across the country. You have to be smarter than this. You have to be more efficient and strategic about what you're doing.

Successful Business Owners Know That the Money Is In The List

For every successful business owner, the long-term and sustainable profits are in having a list of happy past customers to market your offers to.

So if a person calls/walks-in/emails/visits your website or steps into your business, .then you **MUST** make a conscious effort get their contact information. If you fail to do that, you will likely lose that lead forever.

The Next Step...Track Your Leads!

Once you have the long list of happy past customers, the next step is to track your leads. Now, what are the things that you need to track? You need to track which coupon or offer brought them in, how many people come in with them, how they heard about your business, what days the customers come in, and the cost per source. Track the cost per lead. Track everything because you need to know what's working so that you can do more of it or improve on it.

By The Way...

While it's very important to capture the contact information of every person who contacts your business, it's also important to create a separate list of past customers explicitly. You need things like: Name, Address, How much they spent, Birthday, Anniversary, and Children's Birthday's. You need all the things that will be important for you to know in order to send out a timely promotion to them.

By collecting your customer's information, you'll begin to see patterns with your prospective customers like:

- o Name
- o Address
- o How much they spent
- o What they bought
- o What offer or coupon brought them in.
- o Birthday
- o Anniversary

All of these things are very important pieces of information. Once you begin to even use your point of sale system or develop another system for collecting contact information from your customers, you will begin to see trends that you can then use and optimize and maximize to get more sales and get them to come back to your business more often.

Once you get the hang of building your database, you may then proceed to the next level—targeting your customers.

The Next Level

By getting this demographic information, you'll be able to laser target your marketing and advertising to your ideal customer by using things like age, race, marital status, income, hobbies. You will have all the things that resonate with your target market because you have the right information.

Now, once you have your target customers and their contact information which you have gathered from your own database, the next key step to successful marketing is consistent follow up.

New Rule #12 of Business Marketing

You must send weekly or monthly marketing messages to your customer database until they move or die.

The only reason you should collect the contact information of your past customers is so that you can follow up with them regularly and consistently to get them to come back to your business and tell others about your business.

Consistent follow-up is probably the single biggest problem that business owners have. Without consistent follow-up, you leave everything up to chance and the whims and wishes of your customers. You can't chance that.

You need to make sure that every week you have marketing messages going out, whether it's an email or text message or post card, or some other things that you have going out to your customer database. This needs to be like clockwork (i.e. once or twice a week, a couple of times a month). It just needs to be consistent and regular.

New Rule #13 of Business Marketing

You will train your staff on how to politely and naturally lead customers into happily making larger purchases.

Customers in this new economy don't want to be aggressively sold anything, so you need to train your staff to be patiently helpful.

Just because a product or service makes you more profit, doesn't mean that your staffs has to be forceful about offering it to customers. Train your staff to ask leading questions that get customers to reveal their likes and dislikes and then your staff can guide them to a good choice that also makes you more money.

This will ensure that your customers have a pleasant buying experience.

New Rule #14 of Business Marketing

You will train your staff on how to customize what they offer to prospects and their presentations based on the marketing campaign the customer is responding to.

While every customer needs to get the same level of service, you also need to train your staff to discover the reason why the customer visited your business today.

If your staff can find out the marketing piece or offer that brought the prospect or past customer in, then they can begin to offer your products and services that cater to that exact customers' needs and wants. This makes a customer feel connected to your business in a way that can't be accomplished by using a one size fits all approach.

You must approach marketing and running your business in a new way because you're in a very different economy from twenty, ten or even five years ago. In order to succeed in this new economy, you must do things very differently than you've done in the past. You now have a new reality.

This Is About New Beginnings

When we talk about new reality, it means new beginnings... a whole lot of them. New things like the following:

- New Marketing Strategies
- New Overall Focus For Your Business
- New Training For Your Staff
- New Outlook On Your Marketplace
- New Staff (If Needed)

This Is About Building New Habits

When you do new things, you should also start to build new habits. You have to learn from your competitor's successes and failures. Develop a new habit to always, always, always be **asking and listening** to your customers. Learn to take the best ideas from different industries and apply them to your business.

It's Time To Face The Music...

"The market's changed. The taste and expectations of customers have changed. The economy has changed. The question is,

"Why haven't you changed?"

The Old Way:

You're still doing things the old way if you're being the slave of your business and you commonly work 14-18 hours a day. You still haven't changed if you were forced to submit to every whim of every Tom, Dick and Harry that comes into your business because you're desperate for money.

You are still doing things the old ways if you try to sell anything and everything that you can because you're trying to be a one-stop shop business. You're still in the old way if you were wasting tons of money on image ads that brag about how great your business is.

The New Way:

- You're in the new era if there are new customers "finding" your business every day online.

- You have developed a new way of knowing exactly what ad or marketing effort generated every customer who visits your business.

- You are adapting to the new era if you are collecting your customer's contact information so you can notify them of your business's specials, or you are now using technology to attract new customers 24/7.

In this new era, you delegate as much as possible so you can spend your hours working on improving your business instead of working for your business.

It's about enjoying your life and have greater peace of mind knowing you have leveraged the best system to help you get the best possible result.

The One Thing...

What's the one thing that will determine whether or not your business succeeds or fails in this new economy? Is it product quality? Is it customer service? Or is it good staff & support team?

Is it because you have the lowest prices on the block or the best location in town?

WRONG!

*"Your ability to consistently attract new customers and convert them into loyal customers. That is the **number one determinant** of your real business success. – In other words MARKETING!"*

The Secret To Success

The sooner you become the marketer of your business instead of the doer of your business, the faster your income and business will grow!

What Is The New Definition of Marketing?

Marketing is anything that you would do or can do to get customers AND keep customers. Period.

Everything is marketing…and marketing is everything to your success.
Marketing is using…

- Display ads
- Television Commercials
- Newsletters
- Websites
- Flyers
- Postcards
- Yellow Page Ads
- Letterhead
- Business Cards
- Signs
- Billboards
- Loyalty programs

Watch This **FREE** Video Now & Discover A New Era Of Internet Marketing:
www.AndrewCocks.ca

- Every interactions with customers and prospects
- **EVERYTHING IS MARKETING!!!**

Everything that you can do to either get customers or customers or to keep them loyal to your business is marketing!

The Light Comes On...

When you realize that **"everything is marketing..."** your business, the opportunities to marketing your business, looks totally different to you. You see obvious mistakes then you consider how your customers or potential customers might view situations, events or documents.

You will see missed opportunities and a ton of opportunities for improvement when you begin to look at this as everything-has-a-potential-to-be-a marketing message.

No Spray and Pray...

However, **ALL** marketing strategies **MUST** be held accountable to produce profits. This means that you must know the effectiveness of each ad, coupon, letter, flyer, postcard, TV commercial etc.

Your goal is to create a marketing system that's predictable and able to be duplicated. In order to reach that goal, you should be able to know the exact ad that brought every customer into your business.

Bring Friends, Or Else...

Once you are able to create and duplicate a marketing system, your next focus should be on the return on investment.

Every dollar that you spend must come back to your bank account with *at least* 5 new friends to join him. When done correctly, there is no better investment in your business than marketing. Everything else is a cost. You must know your return on investment (ROI) at all times by using direct response marketing.

Direct Response Marketing

Direct Response Marketing is a marketing designed to generate and immediate response or immediate action from a prospect, where each response (and purchase) can be measured, and attributed, and connected to individual advertisements.

Why Direct Response Marketing?

There are a lot of reasons why you should opt for direct response marketing. One, it's personal, specific, clear and simple. It's two-way. It gets your marketing message out but it also lets you know what prompted people to respond or come in and what marketing message got people in to you. (It gets the word back to you so that you know what's working and what's not). Another reason is that it results in a long-term relationship because it's easy to know and track your R.O.I.

In other words, direct response marketing allows you to know exactly what the value of a customers and customer is, because you know exactly what marketing piece brought them in.

Make It Plain & Simple

Start by understanding the benefits your customers wants and offer them it in your ads. Communicate these benefits in an attention-grabbing, compelling and motivating manner. Next, you need to make an offer that has universal appeal to your defined target. Make a soft offer that is non-threatening for potential to respond to.

Make it easy and non-threatening for first-time customers to step into your business and enjoy their first meal. Some business owners offer huge discounts or free coffee to break the ice and create the momentum. When you have the momentum, start to implement tracking mechanisms in your ads that you can test while tracking.

The Direct Response Difference

Using direct response marketing makes your ads and marketing messages much more effective. It starts with an attention grabbing headline that makes a bold and simple to understand claim, promise or offer. The headline qualifies who the remainder of the message/ad is written for. This kind of marketing has ONE clear and simple goal to get the prospective customers to step into your business to get what they want and need.

It also presents a clear call to action. For example, "Tell the employee this phrase…", "Go to this website…", "Bring this coupon in on this date…" etc. Direct response marketing allows you to know the true value and worth of each and every customer.

Coming Up Short

One of the reasons why many business owners have problems with their marketing strategies is because they don't know the value of their customers. When you use direct response marketing and keep an up to date and accurate database of your past customers, you can accurately measure the value of every customer for their lifetime. This is called the lifetime value of a customer.

Lifetime value is how much revenue a customer or customer will bring into your business during their lifetime of dining at your business.

Lifetime Value of a Customer

For example, in order to calculate the lifetime value of your customers, you need to know answers to the following questions:

- Your Average Sale Per Person

- Number of Visits Per Month/Year
- Sales Per Customer Per Year
- Average Number Of People Per Table
- Number of Referrals Per Customer
- The # of Years A Customer Eats At Your Business

If you don't know the answers to these questions then you are at a HUGE disadvantage.

Here is an example:

Your Average Sale Per Person	$35
Number of Visits Per Year	10
Average Number of Years Customer Stays	5
Sales Per Customer Per Year	$350
Number of Referrals Per Customer	3
Gross Sales Over Life Of Customer (5 years)	$1,750
Gross Sales For Total Referrals (5 years)	$5,250

TOTAL VALUE OF A SATISFIED CUSTOMER

Total Value Of 10 Happy Customer	**$7,000**
Total Value Of 100 Happy Customer	$700,000
Total Value Of 1000 Happy Customer	$7,000,000

Most businesses have more than enough customers in their target market to build a 7-figure business or business easily. However, they do little to nothing to get the people to come back and refer others and that's where the problem is.

Lifetime Value of a Customer

The real power and breakthrough in your business will occur when you harness the knowledge of your lifetime value of your customers and use it to implement direct response marketing in all your advertising.

Watch This **FREE** Video Now & Discover A New Era Of Internet Marketing:
www.AndrewCocks.ca

It All Starts To Make Sense

When you realize that the lifetime value of your regular customers is $13,500 over a five year period, giving away a free gift or discount is just a drop in the bucket. Now, all of a sudden you get excited about getting as many of these customers as possible.

Plus, it starts to make sense to consistently run all the marketing strategies you can afford because you know they each represent $13,500 to you in the long term and when you can show your staff that those coupons and inexpensive little gifts actually represent a huge chunk of sales and revenue, they'll finally get the big picture.

CHAPTER 3

Customer Attraction Systems:
How To Stand Head And Shoulders Above Your Competitors While Attracting The Most Profitable Customers

In this chapter you'll discover the easiest and quickest way to motivate the right type of customers to choose your business. We don't want to fill your business with cheap skates. That's not the purpose of this book. We're going to talk about how to create a persuasive and compelling marketing message to your target audience.

I'm going to teach you how to make your business stand head and shoulders above your competitors and how you will always stick out in your customer's minds by giving you proven formulas you can use to make you the clear and obvious choice to your ideal customer.

You're also going to learn the real the truth about the secret way to get people to try your business the first time so that they can get hooked and give you an opportunity to get them as customers.

But first, can you answer this very important question…

Why should a person choose your business over any other and every other business that's available to them, including eating at home?

Trouble In Paradise…

If you struggle to come up with an answer or can't answer that question, then chances are that your business is currently struggling now and you may be on the verge of going out of business soon! That question is that important.

Stand Out Or Sit Down

People won't consistently come to your business if you don't have a compelling reason for them to shop at your business. You may be able to scrape by waiting for walk-in traffic or maybe an ad you run every now and then, but you'll never get to high levels of success without a unique hook, something that speaks to your target prospects and motivates them to get off their couch and come into your business.

The "thing" or "combination of things" that makes your business stand out in your customers mind is called your unique sales proposition (USP). A unique sales proposition can make all the difference for your business. It's the one thing that you have that you become known for or that people associate with your business.

It is also known as...

- Point of difference
- Unique Perceived Benefit
- Unique Selling Point
- Extra Value Proposition
- Competitive Advantage

But regardless of the name, it's the same thing... it's that thing that your business can do, or the experience that you can provide, that is your uniqueness.

I would want you to see the difference between having and not having an effective USP for your business.

Dead In The Water

Not being able to distinguish yourself from your competitors is a curse that will haunt you for as long as your business is open until you address it.

A business with no USP is always at the mercy of the market place, cheap customers or cut throat suppliers. A business with no USP is also ripe for the picking for knockoffs, local competitors and big chain competition. After all, they do the same thing that everyone else does.

Therefore, you need to do something that makes your business unique and makes it stand out in your local marketplace. When you don't have a USP and your supplier prices or operating expenses go up, then you're profits always go down because you don't give your customers any reason why they should pay you one penny more than they're paying you now.

You're In Control

An effective USP gives you the power in every area of your business. You get to pick the exact customer or customer you want. You get the power to set your own terms. You get the power to charge higher prices. You can dictate your terms to your suppliers because you deliver them so much business. You get to choose your busiest days or down time.

In short, your business is back under your control because you have this thing that can't be duplicated. You have this experience or ambiance that no one else can do the way that you do it and so you can demand a premium for it.

It Gets Even Better

A really good USP does more than just get you customers. It also sets the strategic direction for your business. It lets everyone know what to expect from your business. Your USP is not simply a marketing or advertising "thing".

A compelling USP is more than a headline at the top of your ads. Your USP is the backbone of your business. A good USP is more valuable than any marketing gimmick, newspaper ad or flyer. In essence, it's your entire business.

Effective USP Essentials

This is what you need to make a really good USP that stands out on your customer's mind.

Each advertisement must make a relevant appealing offer to the customer or customer. This is the first step. It can't just be shallow words or purely advertising. The advertisement must tell the customer that if you come to business, you will get this specific result or benefit.

The offer you're making in your advertisement must be something that your competition cannot or does not or is not willing to offer. It must be unique in some way that makes it stand out in the minds of your target market. The offer must be so compelling that it can get people to get up off their couches right now and come to your business today.

But, don't make a mistake of trying to compete on low price alone. As you build better USP's and you get a proven track record for delivering on your USP, you should be raising your prices.
That's the trade-off. It's what you strive to do. You strive to become so unique.

How Many USP's Do You Need?

There are two groups of USP's that you will have to create:

1. **USP Group #1:** This is your overall business USP that focuses on the general experience or expectations a customer should have when they reach your business.

2. **USP Group #2:** This is the USP you create for each specific ad, special, promotion, product or service that you offer.

Yes, you need both types of USP's for your business to stand out in the minds of your target market.

Bad & Ineffective USP's

While a good USP can help your business consistently break sales records and grow profits, a bad USP can repel the exact customers you're trying to attract.

Here are some examples:

- You have been in business for X amount of years. People really don't care about that anymore like they used to
- Or we have the lowest price for whatever you sell once again that's a great way to go out of business in a few months
- Next we have every type of widget. This is about standing out there are a lot of different places that carry a lot of different products you want to stand out in your customers mind for what you do really well.
- And things like satisfaction guaranteed which really doesn't mean much to any one at this point in time.
- And other like we are the best _____ in town

All customers hear when you use things like that is blah blah blah blah it doesn't really mean anything to the customer.

Overall Business U.S.P's That Sell

Watch This **FREE** Video Now & Discover A New Era Of Internet Marketing:
www.AndrewCocks.ca

Let's take a look at two examples of industries that have USPs that sell:

- Fed-Ex: When it absolutely, positively has to be there next day. When you had a high priority document that you needed to get somewhere overnight, you choose Fedex.

- Raymour & Flanigan: 3 Day delivery guaranteed.
  They have guaranteed delivery of your furniture in 3 days or less. They were the first furniture retailer in New England to offer 3 day delivery, so if you needed it fast, you choose Raymour & Flanigan.

- Domino's: Delivery in 30 minutes or its free.
  If you were hungry and needed pizza fast, then you chose Domino's. Notice that they didn't say good pizza. They're just talking about 30 minutes and it's a fast pizza. So, you chose Domino's.

What Do All Those USP's Have In Common?

Well, they were in high competition industries and business. They spoke to their target market with their USPs. Most target a niche within a niche. Not everyone wants fast pizzas, some people want pizza that tastes delicious. Not everyone wants furniture in 3 days, some people want custom furniture. So, they spoke to their market places. It was usually a niche within a niche.

All were regular, boring products like furniture, mail delivery, and pizza. There was nothing special about the industries on the examples I just gave you. They were things that you could use right away.

The "It" Factor That Made ALL Those USP's Work!

They were precise enough to echo the prospects' thoughts. So if you're sitting at home and you wanted something to quickly eat without cooking, you chose Domino's. They were guaranteeing either it's 30 minutes or it's free. It echoed in your thoughts so you then set your clock, and it became a game.

USP's work because they address the biggest objection or fear to buying. If you were in the market for furniture and you came across Raymour & Flanigan's ads, you definitely paid attention. After all, there's nothing worse than paying thousands of dollars for furniture and having to wait and you got your in-laws coming in town but you have to wait six months when you wanted it in 3 days or less.

They also promise to solve one problem that the prospect will pay to have solved. If you wanted something overnight and you were willing to pay that premium to Fed-Ex to get it there overnight, that wasn't a big problem.

It includes the dominant emotion driving the prospect. You wanted it fast and you needed it quick—dominant emotions.

It's unique enough to be easily memorable. Most business owners don't have the guts to make strong guarantees. It's just what it is. But if Fed-Ex did it... if Domino's did it... if Raymour & Flanigan did it, you can do it too!

You just have to be creative and you have to take the time to make sure that you can deliver on your promise yet it's a worthwhile investment.

CHAPTER 4

Million Dollar Marketing Messages: Marketing Messages That Consistently Fill Your Business With High Quality Leads And Eager Prospects

Most business owners waste tens of thousands of dollars on ads, flyers and marketing strategies that never have a chance of being successful. Sadly, the reason why their ads and marketing don't work is because the business owners are allowing ad reps to create the ads and offers. Also, in most cases, the ad reps only recommend extreme discounting as the only thing that's working in today's market. And nothing could be further from the truth.

If you had to take a guess, who do you think knows the customers and customer at your business better than you and your staff? Nobody does! That's why you, along with the input of your staff who understand your vision and customers, should be the ones creating your ads, offers and marketing messages.

The Necessary Ingredient

As a business owner, you must know how to create simple but effective marketing messages that attract the right type of customers to your business. There is no excuse for you as the business owner not knowing how to create marketing messages that attract customers. If you don't do it and if you don't know it, who does know it and who will do it?

The truth is that being able to create marketing messages is just as important as any other skill in your business. In fact, without knowing how to create marketing messages that consistently attract customers, you're always just one bad month or quarter away from going out of business. Stop living on the edge. You need to know how to write simple but effective marketing messages.

It's Not Rocket Science

You don't have to become a professional writer or a graphic designer in order to create great marketing resources that generate customers. You don't need a fancy computer, college degree or expensive software to make good ads for your business.

Some of the best ads and offers were written using a pen and a napkin. You just have to be willing to spend a few hours a week writing down new and different ways to get the attention of your target market and your past customers.

It's no different than coming up with ideas for new products or services you can offer. You just need a few core ingredients and you can do any number of different things to give it a unique twist.

What Is A Marketing Message?

A marketing message is any ad, flyer, email, tweet, postcard or anything else you can use to communicate your offer to prospective customers or to past customers which encourage them to come back to your business.

Coming up with a good effective marketing message is not some complicated, confusing thing that will take you twenty years to learn. If you can talk to customers that you have and you can, then you can write effective marketing messages for your business.

Simply put, writing a marketing message is your ability to write on paper what you've already been saying to friends and family to get them to come to your business.

The Core of The Problem

Without having a proven system for creating good offers, ads and marketing messages, most business owners have little to no chance of succeeding long term. In fact, most business owners are doing their marketing completely backwards.

- They are advertising to the worst possible target markets
- In the most expensive and least effective places
- Making the worst possible offers
- To people that couldn't care less
- While ignoring the best possible customers!

Let's break it down and examine each marketing mistake.

Marketing Problem #1:

Advertising to the worst possible target market.

If you ask the average business owner who is his target market, he would answer you by saying that anybody with a pulse. However, the fact of the matter is that only a certain percentage of the population in your area will ever buy the type of product or service that you sell.

Therefore, the worst possible target market is people who have not shown any particular interest in your business or the type of product or service that you sell. These are people who are just not interested in anything you have to offer them and you should not waste any time with them.

It's ridiculous to think that every single person will like what you're offering. Yet, most business owners think everyone is their target market. That's completely wrong and that's why they waste thousands of dollars trying to market to everybody.

Marketing Problem #2:

Advertising in the most expensive and least effective places.

The second big marketing mistakes committed by business owners is advertising in the most expensive and ineffective places. There was a day and a time when your local yellow pages, newspaper, radio and television stations would get you all the customers you would ever need. That day has come and it has gone

Now, the big four: yellow pages, newspaper, radio and television are little more than a waste of money for the majority of business owners. That's not to say that you wouldn't get any customers from marketing in them, but there are places to advertise that are less expensive and more effective.

At the end of the day, you shouldn't be advertising anywhere that your ideal target market doesn't hang out. And if you don't know that your target market is using the yellow pages or reading the newspapers or listening to certain radio stations or viewing certain television stations then you shouldn't be advertising you should only be advertising where your ideal target market will see and will have a great chance of seeing your marketing message.

So, Where Should You Advertise These Days?

Well In today's digital age, there are more places to advertise than ever before, but the least expensive and most effective marketing strategies are the ones that only target your ideal customers. For example:

- Sending an email or text message to a past customer for your "past customer only" offer costs less than one cent each.

- Showing your ads on Facebook for less than $5-$10 per day to people who have shown an interest in the product or services your business offers.

- Sending out targeted postcards or letters to people in your town for 50 cents per letter or postcard who have bought it at other businesses just like yours recently.

There are dozens of ways to only invest your marketing dollars with people who have already demonstrated that they would be willing to eat at your business. That's where you should be advertising in this day and age.

Marketing Problem #3:

Making the worst possible offers when you're advertising.

The worst possible offer is the one that doesn't get any of your ideal target market to come into your business or an offer that attracts the type of customers that you don't want. While you should give all customers that walk through your door the same quality of service, you must acknowledge that many people who walk through your door are not your ideal customer.

It doesn't make you a bad person. It just makes you a smart business owner and marketer. Your goal is to attract your ideal target market with your offers. Also, most business owners think that lowering their prices is the only offer that will work to get new people in the door but that's not true. More important, if you only use price discounts to get customers then you are training your customers to only buy when you are lowering your prices. That's a terrible and dangerous way to run your business

So, What Are The Best Type of Offers?

Your offer is the heart and soul of your marketing efforts. Without a good offer, nothing you say or do in your ad will matter. Therefore the best type of offers are the offers that attract that attract your ideal target market and get them to come in and spend more money, visit more frequently and generate more referrals.

What Offers Does Your Target Market Want?

Every type of target market will respond differently to various offers. Your goal after you figure out your target markets is to begin to come up with offers that appeal to them in a persuasive way.

The best way to figure out what your customers or clients want is to consistently ask them and to look at your past sales receipts. If you're completely lost about how to create offers, then look at your receipts for what your customers are already purchasing.

That will give you crystal clarity about what they value or want more of. This will become easier for you to do as you begin to practice this more often.

Marketing Problem #4:

Advertising and marketing to people that couldn't care less.

No matter how great your products and services are at your business, there are people who will never do business with you. You shouldn't waste one penny advertising to those types of people because it's a huge waste of resources.

Most business owners will never even acknowledge that these types of people exist. They mistakenly think that everybody is their potential target market. For example:

- If you own an Italian business that bases 99% of your dishes around meat-based sauces, you have no business advertising to vegetarians, or
- If you own a women's clothing store business, then you should never advertise to men unless your offer is focused on men buying clothes for the women in their lives – otherwise you'll likely waste a ton of money to get a few meager sales

When you see these statements in writing, it seems obvious doesn't it? But, are you doing just that in your marketing?

So, Who Would Most Enjoy Your Business?

Through technology, you can laser target your marketing messages to people who have either expressed their interest in the exact type of product or service you offer or they've shopped at a business like yours before.

There's no reason why you should waste thousands of dollars on mass advertising methods where 98% of the marketing messages are sent to the wrong people. Credit card companies sell lists of people in your town and area who've already shopped at businesses like yours. You can then send those people postcards, letters or flyers and get a much better return.

Facebook also allows you to target your ads to people who have stated that they like the exact type of products, services and experience your business offers. There are dozens of strategies that allow you to only focus on people who would be most likely to shop at your business. That's what you should be doing.

Marketing Problem #5:

Marketing while ignoring the best possible customers!

Most business owners spend all of their marketing dollars trying to get new customers, but spend little to no money on the best type of customer. **And just so we're clear:** The best type of customer is the customer that has already bought from your business before.

You should spend just as much money marketing to get your past customers to come back to your business as you do to people who've never shopped at your business before. After all, your past customers are the ones who are the easiest to convince to come back to your business and will be most willing to refer others to you.

So, you should also have specific marketing strategies that are designed to keep your past customers coming back to your business in addition to getting new customers.

CHAPTER 5

Website & Internet Marketing Strategy: Using The Power Of The Internet To Increase Your Sales And Profits

In this chapter it's all about using your website and your internet to fill the tables at your business. In this chapter you will discover how to dominate your competitors and own your target market using only the internet and free online tools. I will show you how you can build a super profitable business marketing plan using only local marketing strategies in your target market and I will reveal the proven formula for online marketing success for your business by giving five online marketing strategies that you must use in order to dominate your market place.

The Great Leveler

A savvy business owner can dominate their target market with just a simple website, free Twitter account, free YouTube account and a free Facebook page. The Internet has leveled the playing field and opened up the door for the business owner with a small marketing budget to compete for a large market share. Never in the history of the world has life-changing success for your business be so easily accessible.

However, the true power isn't simply because a business has a website or social media accounts on the Internet, it's about using your website, social media and the internet to get people to come eat at your business.

Online Marketing Myths

Now although marketing online can dramatically change your business, some business owners believe several myths about marketing online that are simply not true.

1. **Myth #1:** They believe that marketing online is too complicated and expensive for business owner's to do.
2. **Myth #2:** All you need is a website and you are guaranteed to instantly get tons of people to come to your business. Nothing can be further from the truth.
3. **Myth #3:** They believe that you need to spend a fortune on a very expensive website to get people to visit their website and their business
4. **Myth #4:** If your website is on the first page of Google, then their business will be flooded with customers.
5. **Myth #5:** Marketing on the internet can solve all your advertising and marketing problems. And this things simply aren't true
6. **Myth #6:** All you need is a Facebook page and a twitter account and you'll automatically get more customers. That's another common misconception.

These myths are holding many business owners back from truly succeeding in their businesses by using the power of the internet. However, even when business owners attempt to market their business online, many still fail. Here are the major reasons why that happen:

Why 99% of Business Owners Fail

- They don't focus on the leads and prospects in their local market. Also known as local search.
- They don't have a major strategy to guide their actions. They just have a random set of marketing actions with no plan.
- They don't understand how to create online marketing campaigns that drive people to their business.
- They don't tie their internet marketing actions and strategies with their traditional successful business strategy systems.
- They don't track results, so there's no way to know what is and isn't working.

Don't Ignore The Truth

In order to be successful with your online marketing efforts, you need to accept the truth about marketing your business online. See, people love to talk online about their experience at your business. So, that means that people are now using social media sites like Facebook and Twitter and review sites like Urban-spoon and Yelp to share their opinions of your business online. This means that your potential customers are also using these same places to see what other people are saying about you. You would have to be crazy to ignore these new trends.

Sit Up And Pay Attention

That's why it's important that you first setup, monitor and maintain your website, social media webpages and review websites. At the end of the day, what others say about your business, whether good or bad, has a big impact on whether potential customers will give your business a shot.

~ 71 ~

However, if you don't update, monitor or maintain your online reputation and resources, you're going to lose out on hundreds and possibly thousands of potential customers. Plus, it's also important for you to have a good grasp of online marketing so that you can track and monitor the results of your online marketing strategies. Let's about competition which is quite tough in this market.

Competition Is Fierce

As an independent business owner, you are in a dogfight for customers when you market online because big chains are many times more likely to provide all of the online things that your customers and customer want. Things like: purchasing gift cards, downloading coupons and promotions. Even worse, chains are nearly ten times more likely to have a mobile website than independent business owners are.

That's why you have to have a game plan for turning tweets, posts and reviews into paying customers. You can't simply throw some stuff up and think it will work. You have to understand the consumers and customers in your area market.

Right In Your Backyard

See, most business owners want a website and a Facebook page so that they can become a big brand and be famous. But, it takes more than just a Facebook page and a few tweets here and there to get more customers your business. The fact of the matter is that there are more than enough customers within 5-10 miles of your business to fuel a high six or seven figure business for you. But that's only possible if you take the time to create a good plan to consistently market your business online in your local area.

It's been tested and proven that localized online and mobile ads are perceived by consumers as more relevant and drive more responses.

Local Online Marketing

In fact local-based marketing strategies make a huge difference in online and mobile ad response. In recent studies, when people were asked what variables or factors would cause them to respond to ads, mobile users said the following:

- Ads that are locally relevant to them by smartphones 73% and tablet 70%
- Ads that offer coupons and promotions by smartphones 72% tablet and 69%
- Ads from known brands: 59% on tablets and 65% on smartphones

The study also found that 66 % of mobile device owners noticed ads, while 33% clicked on mobile ads. So you have to have online presence and have good marketing strategy.

They're Ready To Buy

More importantly than just opening and clicking on ads, people who are searching for a local business with their smart phones and tablets are searching in order to make a quick decision. According to a recent study, 64% of smartphone and 44% of tablet users searching for businesses make a decision within an hour to 24 hours of doing their research. If you think it through, it makes perfect sense. People who are searching on their phones and tablets are most likely in their car or on the road. So, if you don't have a well-thought out online presence and marketing strategy, you're missing out on a steady stream of customers who are ready to make a decision within an hour of 24 hours of doing searches online. With this information you simply can't ignore the value of mobile advantage.

The Mobile Advantage

The next thing to note is that 70 percent of total time spent with business content on mobile devices took place in apps. In other words, people are spending much more time looking for business options on mobile applications:

- 81% of consumers surveyed have searched for a business on a mobile app in the last 6 months.
- 92% of those surveyed have searched for a business on the web in the last 6 months.
- 75% of consumers surveyed often choose a business to dine at based on search results of when they searched.
- And 84% of consumers look at more than one business before choosing where they want to shop.

What Matters To Them?

Studies have also shown that three out of five people who are searching for a business on a mobile device don't have a specific place in mind when they start their search. In other words, they're searching for somewhere to go that looks like it might have good food and a good experience. And the main criteria that impacted what business they chose was the following:

- Location or proximity — so 65% of Smartphone Users and 52% of Tablet Users were focused on location or proximity to where they were searching from
- The Price — about 48% of Smartphone Users and about the same amount of Tablet Users were focused on price
- And then 27% of smartphone users versus 43% of tablet users were focused on the good reviews that were online about the business or potential location they were going to.

Does It Matter?

As indicated, the top activities among business searchers varied by device. Among smartphone owners the hierarchy of activities was the following:

1. Calling a business.
2. Looking up directions.
3. Looking up directions for businesses near them.

Tablet owners were much more interested in "research mode" and were more likely to do the following:

- Look at ratings and reviews.
- Find online coupons and promotions.
- 3rd research for specific products and services.

So if you look at these two different categories you are going to see that smartphone users were focused on calling a business which makes sense as they are on their phone. Then, they were secondarily concerned with looking at their directions to the business they called. Lastly, they were concerned with looking up directions to businesses that were near them. Meanwhile tablet owners were looking to do a little more research to find out a little more about their business.

Just Another Tool

Many independent business owners get stressed out over how rapidly the Internet changes and how they can best use it to promote their business. The first thing you need to keep in mind about using the Internet to grow your business sales is that the Internet is just a tool for you to use in your business marketing toolbox. Don't get overwhelmed by all the options and new websites, software and programs that are coming out every day. You must have a simple plan that you create once, review each week and update about once per month and then stick to it. In other words, you need a plan that you consistently follow and implement.

Online Marketing Formula For Businesses

The ideal plan for generating customers from the Internet doesn't have to be complicated. However, you must follow a specific set of steps in order to do it successfully. Here are the steps.

1. **You need to map out your process** – This includes mapping out your entire process for working with a prospect generated from any source on the internet.

2. **You need to identify your target prospect** - In order for any marketing or business growth strategy to work, you have to first have to know who you're trying to get or who you are trying to attract to your business

3. **You need to create your offer-** Once you attract prospects to your website or social media webpage, you need to have one or more compelling and persuasive offers to get them into your business quickly.

4. **Attracting the prospects - T**his is all about selecting online marketing strategies that gets your offer in front of your target prospects.

5. **Lead Capture** – This is your method for getting prospects to give you their contact information in exchange of the offer or good that they are going to get.

6. **Cultivating Your Leads** – These are your tactics for building a relationship with your database of contacts over time in order to make your offer and then in order to get them into your business quickly

Follow The Plan

Following this proven blueprint eliminates the guesswork, confusion and dramatically eliminates the risk of major failure of your marketing efforts. You will grow to love following up with the leads that are generated from your online marketing efforts because you have a proven blueprint to convert them into paying customers. More importantly, your customers will enjoy coming to your business and will become raving fans.

************** Exclusive Offer **************

Would You Like Me To Design A Custom Marketing Campaign For You, For Free?

From The Desk Of Andrew Cocks

Dear Friend,

I've set aside some time to design a custom marketing campaign for you, personally.

I'll meet with you live using Google Hangout and **literally design a customized marketing campaign specifically for your business.**

Once it's designed, **I'll then build you a blueprint/process map of it so you'll be able to deploy it at will.**

Watch This **FREE** Video Now & Discover A New Era Of Internet Marketing:
www.AndrewCocks.ca

Here's How It Works

We begin working before we ever meet.

We analyze your target market, spy on your competitors, and play "mystery shopper" by going through your sales process as if we were a potential prospect.

Then We Meet, One-On-One.

We'll do it using Google Hangout so we can share the screen with you as we design your campaign (and build your blueprint for you) in real time.

Everything is done custom and is built specifically for your business after we've had a chance to ask you about your sales process, your sales goals, and your branding strategy.

There Is No Charge For This and There Is No Catch.

...Which of course leads you to wonder, *"Why would you do all of this work for free"?*

Well, in the interest of full transparency, this is how I get clients.

A good percentage of the people I do this for end up asking me to actually **build all of their marketing campaigns *for* them.**

When that happens, my in-house team and I actually build all the web pages, build the follow-up campaigns, and implement everything *for* the client.

Watch This **FREE** Video Now & Discover A New Era Of Internet Marketing:
www.AndrewCocks.ca

So that's my "hidden motivation" for doing this.

However...

This Is NOT
A "Sales Pitch In Disguise".

Far from it. *You'll get no pressure to become a client* because I let the value of the free work speak for itself.

The campaign I design for you, *for free*, will be absolutely transformational for your business.

I guarantee it.

But anyone could say that, couldn't they?

Which is why I'm willing to make you this promise:

I'll Give You My $200.00 Product Launch Secrets Program If You Don't Like It.

If you tell me that I've wasted your time during our conversation, **I'll immediately give you my $200.00 Product Launch Secrets Program** to compensate you for the hour or so we spend together.

There's no "fine print" here. No "catch".

The bottom line is, I'll design you an amazing marketing campaign for free and I'll even give you a blueprint of it so you can deploy it at once.

Watch This **FREE** Video Now & Discover A New Era Of Internet Marketing:
www.AndrewCocks.ca

After that, you might want to become a client. Or not. *I won't pressure you either way.*

And if you think I wasted your time, I'll give you my $200.00 Product Launch Secrets Program.

If you'd like a free customized marketing campaign and blueprint, then visit the website address below to get started.

✱✱✱✱✱✱✱✱✱✱✱✱✱✱✱✱✱✱✱✱✱✱✱✱✱

www.AndrewCocks.ca/free

✱✱✱✱✱✱✱✱✱✱✱✱✱✱✱✱✱✱✱✱✱✱✱✱✱

CHAPTER 6

Loyalty Marketing Systems:
How To Practically Guarantee That Your
Customers Buy From You For Life!

The easiest customer to close is a past customer who already knows, likes and trusts you because they've bought from you before. Think about it. Who would you rather call or send a marketing message to? A past customer that has already purchased from you previously or someone you've never met, to whom you'll have to explain your product or service and convince them it's got value and that you are a trustworthy and reputable business?

Satisfaction Is Nearly Worthless

In the good old days most business owners focused on satisfying their customers, but after hundreds of thousands of customers were surveyed, it was discovered that:

- Satisfied customers rarely refer anyone to a business and often purchase from direct competitors of the business they claim to be satisfied with.
- Loyal customers tell everyone about the business without even being prompted AND always shop at the business they're loyal to.
- Loyal customers proactively look for other customers for you and encourage them to visit your business.

So the moral of the story is that you want loyal customers who buy from you over and over. That's how you'll know they're satisfied.

That's why you should invest just as much money and resources in keeping your past customers as you do in getting new customers. In other words you should focus on creating customer loyalty in your company.

The Customer Loyalty Advantage

A loyal customer is someone who loves buying products and services from you because they enjoy their buying experience with your company. They are loyal to your company because your service is exceptional because the reality is there are likely dozens of places where they can get a product like yours but they stay loyal because your service is exceptional.

They are also loyal to you because they believe that they're receiving much more in value than the price they're paying. They are also loyal to you because they trust that when a problem comes up, you'll exceed their expectations in how you solve that problem. In short they trust you.

So, because they are loyal to you, they tell their friends, family members and even complete strangers about your company because they want to introduce people to your great products and services.

In short, customer loyalty is the ultimate reward that you receive because you consistently provide above average products and services and you know how to resolve problems and issues at an exceptional level. However, never forget that customer loyalty is a behavior, activity or process. The customer must be consistently doing something (preferably buying something from you) to be considered loyal.

Loyalty Has Its Privileges

While the most obvious benefit to having fiercely loyal customers is the increase in sales and profits, there are dozens of other benefits like:

- They buy in larger quantities.
- They give you valuable feedback in a non-threatening way to improve your business.
- They tend to interact in a more positive way with your staff, creating a better "vibe" in your business.
- They tend not to explode on you when simple little mistakes happen.
- They're more responsive to your marketing efforts.

The list goes on and on, but I'm going to share the top seven benefits for you so that you know the immediate impact they'll have on your bottom line right away.

Loyal Customer Benefit #1: You generate profit.

Getting new customers is expensive. Most companies don't know their true customer acquisition costs because they have never added up all of the costs of getting new customers. Costs like paying salespeople, marketing agencies, advertising, website, marketing salaries, promotional items just to name a few.

See if you add up all of these expenses and divide the total by the number of new customers obtained during that period, you'll get the true cost of getting a new customer. If you were to do this

Watch This **FREE** Video Now & Discover A New Era Of Internet Marketing:
www.AndrewCocks.ca

exercise, what you'd find is that don't actually make a profit from a customer until they have purchased a second or perhaps even a third time. That's why loyalty generates most of the profits.

Loyal Customer Benefit #2: They buy more from you.

In most cases, the first purchase is a test to see if buying from you works out well and makes the customer happy. He wants to see if you're reliable, he wants to see of you are hassle free, and can make and keep your promise. The second time he buys, he's looking to make sure this buying experience is repeatable and trustworthy.

By the third time, he actually becomes a customer because he knows that his needs will be met and that it will be a pleasant and positive experience. He now trusts you and may be ripe to purchase more from you and at a higher price point.

Therefore, you now have the opportunity to cross-sell and up-sell because your customer is comfortable enough to try new things you recommend. In short, you are now a trusted vendor.

Loyal Customer Benefit #3: They send you referrals.

Customers who are delighted with your product or service can't wait to spread the word to colleagues or friends. Word of mouth is the least expensive and most cost-effective customer acquisition strategy.

It can also be the most powerful because the relationships that the customer has with the people he refers foster an added level of trust for your business. This is especially true today. People share their best and worst experiences on social media websites like Facebook, Twitter, Pinterest, Yelp, YouTube, and other social media networks or blogs - not just in writing, but also with photos and videos. This organic and unsolicited word-of-mouth referral from a loyal customer is worth its weight in gold.

Loyal Customer Benefit #4: They're not as price sensitive.

Loyal customers are not only looking at the purchase price. They expect and want a great buying experience coupled with their product or services. Plus it's been found that they are willing to pay extra for your company's product or service to get personal recognition and an individualized experience. This allows you to charge a premium price for a premium experience, service and product. This also increases your profits exponentially because it allows you make more profit per sale with little to no increase in your costs.

It's also been proven that customers who pay a premium price often experience a higher level of satisfaction with their purchase purely based on the price they paid.

Loyal Customer Benefit #5: They pay you on time

Loyal customers help your business thrive by paying on time, which provides you with steady, stable and predictable cash flow. Your faithful customers love what you offer, buy regularly, and pay when expected because they are happy with their purchase. This allows you to count on a steady, predictable cash flow from which you can pay your expenses and subsequently reinvest in your business.

There are many businesses that have more money tied up in outstanding receivables than they have actually flowing into their coffers. If none of the other benefits of customer loyalty resonate with you, this should definitely be worth working towards building a loyalty-inducing business.

Loyal Customer Benefit #6: They become your competitive advantage

The increase in sales and profits that loyal customers bring to your business allow you the cash flow to upgrade every area of your business. Over time this advantage begins to compound and with the right amount of strategic planning and implementing you have happier employees, better products and services and better marketing. But it also means that you have the resources to enhance your product/service and customer experience even more.

It will reach a point where any prospect or regular customer that comes in contact with your business will begin to notice the difference. This continuous improvement inevitably results in your company taking market share away from your competitors.

Loyal Customer Benefit #7: They are more forgiving of mistakes

Every business owner has been in a situation where product was damaged, service was incomplete or any number of issues arose. However, when you're dealing with a loyal client or customer they will be more likely to accept your apology and the "fix," and then move on from there.

This usually happens because they look at your company from the point of view of caring and trust, so as long as they're handled correctly, the mistakes have less significance. In fact, it's these very mistakes and issues that give you a chance to demonstrate to your customers that you go above and beyond when issues come up.

The speed and quality of your fix creates a "wow" factor and gives you a chance to turn a problem into a positive story for your testimonials and successes.

However, The Fact of The Matter Is...

Despite all the numerous benefits of creating loyal customers, most businesses spend 100% of their marketing budget to only get new customers. Then, once they get a new customer, they immediately divorce the customer and act as if they never existed. Instead businesses should be working to develop a lasting and profitable relationship with the customer who has voted with the money.

Loyalty Doesn't Just Happen

Customer loyalty doesn't just happen by accident while you're going along the course of running your business. In fact, it's been proven that a regular customer goes through several stages before they become loyal:

1. **Stage 1: Suspect** - A suspect is anyone who might possibly buy your product or service. We call them suspects because we believe, or "suspect," they might buy, but we don't know enough yet to be sure.
2. **Stage 2: Prospect** - A prospect is someone who has a need for your product or service and is able to buy. Although a prospect has not yet purchased from you, he may have heard about you, read about you or had someone recommend you to him. Prospects may know who you are, where you are and what you sell, but they still haven't bought from you.

3. **Stage 3: Disqualified Prospects** - Disqualified prospects are those prospects who do not need, or do not have the ability to buy, your products or services.
4. **Stage 4: First-Time Customer** - A first-time customer is one who has already purchased from you just that one time.
5. **Stage 5: Repeat Customer** - Repeat customers are people who have purchased from you two or more times. They may have bought the same product twice or bought two different products or services on two or more occasions.

6. **Stage 6: Advocate** - An advocate buys everything you have to sell that they can possibly use and purchases regularly from you. In addition, however, an advocate encourages other to buy from you.

Laws Of Building Customer Loyalty.

There are several important business principles that you need to be aware of that will determine how successful you can become at building customer loyalty in your business.

1. **Your focus on building staff loyalty.** - Loyal customers want relationships and familiarity. They want to buy from people who know them and their preferences. It's virtually impossible to build strong customer loyalty with a high rate of staff turnover.

2. **Know where the money comes from.** - All customers are not created equal. Roughly speaking, 80% of your revenue is being generated by 20% of your customers. Some customer spend more and thus they represent more long-term value to your company than other customers. That's why you need to pay especially close attention to the high-value customers.

3. **Know the loyalty stages.** Customers become loyal to a company and its products and service one step at a time. By understanding the customer's current loyalty stage, you can better determine what's necessary to move that customer to the next level.

4. **You can't just sell all the time. Serve them.** Today's customers are smarter, better informed and more intolerant of "being sold" than ever before. They expect doing business with you to be as hassle-free and gratifying for

them as possible. They believe that you earn their business with service that is pleasant, productive and personalized.

5. **Look for customer complaints.** In most companies 90% of customer complaints are unarticulated and manifest themselves in many negative ways like: unpaid invoices, lack of courtesy to staff etc. You need to make it easy for customers to complain, and then take those complaints seriously by addressing them and fixing them.

6. **Be available for your customers.** Customers associate your responsiveness and availability to their perception of good service. Technology tools such as customer self-service, email management and live chat/Web callback are becoming mandatory.

7. **See your value from customers' perspective.** Knowing how your customers experience value and then delivering on those terms is critical to building strong customer loyalty. Keep in mind that customers' value definitions are constantly changing. That's why you must stay tuned in to your customers.

8. **Win back lost customers.** The average business loses 20-40% of its customers every year, which is why it's important that you have a strategy for getting your past loyal customers to come back to you. After all, research shows that a business is twice as likely to successfully sell to a lost customer as to a new prospect

However the sad reality is that every business doesn't deserve loyal customers. See your worthiness to expect loyalty depends on your ability to consistently meet and exceed your customers' expectations.

Most companies have no problem meeting the bare minimum standard that customers use to make a purchase decision. However, very few companies exceed those minimum standards. That's why you need to honestly evaluate how your company is interacting and engaging with your customers. You can get the best information by either secretly shopping your own business or hire a mystery shopper to get an honest perspective from your customers view point.

Standout Or Sit Down

Standout customer service is the foundation upon which you build your customer loyalty. No standout customer = no widespread customer loyalty. When you view every customer interaction as critical to building customer loyalty, it instantly makes clear what the correct solution to the situation should be. But at the end of the day, it is your level of customer service—the way your business treats and values customers.

Also, it's nearly impossible to talk about customer loyalty without talking about customer service. All business owners know that without customers they don't have a business which is why they spend so much money to get customers. However, their business systems and processes don't always reflect a "customer first" mentality. That doesn't mean the customer is always right, but it means that you'll always do right by your customers because they ultimately determine your success.

The Key Principles of Customer Service That Lead To Customer Loyalty

Customer Service Principle 1: Your customer signs your paycheck.

Don't be fooled by the signature at the bottom of your payroll check -- the guy who signed the check didn't put the money there -- your customers did.

No customers, no money. Your business is worthless, and your wallet is empty without funds provided by customers. The more you work for the customer's success, the more you will earn. It's just that simple.

Customer Service Principle 2: Customers want help with something.

The only reason customers are contacting you is because they want some kind of help with something. That could be help with solving a problem, help with using or understanding a product or service they purchased or help with something else. If you gain their trust, they won't call the competition and they won't be as price sensitive. They just want help and comfort. That's why you need to know why your customers are call, visiting or contacting you while also focusing on the best way to respond to each of their needs

Customer Service Principle 3: Be your best on every customer interaction.

Generally speaking every customer is worth 20+ times the size of their annual purchase amounts when you factor in referrals and multiple purchases. That's why it's important to invest just as much money and energy to keep them as you do to get them in the first place. Every customer contact is an opportunity to earn the next sale. You must impress upon your staff the importance of treating every customer like they're the most important person in the world because they are at that moment in time.

Customer Service Principle 4: Focus on building a good relationship.

~ 91 ~

It's a common fact that a loyal customer is a powerful competitive advantage, but it requires you to have a good relationship with them. The quality of the relationship with your customers determines whether they'll keep buying over and over again more than the price of your products. That's why you should spend some time with relationship building strategies instead of only using sales techniques. Stay in front of your customer in times of "non-sale" as much as you do in times of a sale.

Customer Service Principle 5: Word of mouth is priceless.

Research has shown that word of mouth advertising is 50 times more powerful than advertising. While it shouldn't be the only advertising you rely on, it would be foolish to ignore the effectiveness of word of mouth advertising. Therefore, you have to acknowledge that great customer service is the only way to create favorable word-of-mouth-advertising. After all, people will believe your other customers in situations where they'd never completely trust your company.

Don't Leave It To Chance

While great customer service is the foundation upon which you build customer loyalty, it does require something more to convert suspects into advocates. Primarily you want to combine great customer service with an incentive based program to motivate your past customers to be loyal with their actions. Keep in mind that customer loyalty is based on actions and not "feelings". You only consider a customer loyal if they come back and buy from you time and time again.

CHAPTER 7

Referral Marketing Systems:
How To Generate Massive Sales And Profits By Getting Referrals From Your Customers & Local Businesses

Referrals are a gravy train that you should do everything in your power to consistently get. However, like most successful business building strategies, it takes real work and real changes, so many business owners avoid it like the plague.

To be honest with you, the large majority of business owners don't have a single system in place to generate referrals.

Missing The Boat

Getting referrals is great because you can get hundreds of people to visit your business at little to no additional cost. Plus, it's less expensive to generate referrals from existing customers than trying to get new customers. Referrals don't have to be convinced to come to your business because they've already been pre-sold on coming by other customers. When you create a referral marketing system, it's a strategic line that partners you with your past customers but you also create an awesome customer environment that builds customer royalty.

<h2 style="text-align:center">Why Most Business Owners Are Not Worthy
Of Receiving Referrals</h2>

- They have no real commitment to getting referrals.
- There's too much focus on selfish reasons.
- They don't even remember to ask for referrals.
- They are really not doing something unique or different that customers can recommend to other people.
- Assuming that a great service alone is enough.
- Being afraid of asking for referrals.

The Golden Road

1. Level 1: Attracting people to your business
2. Level 2: Converting to loyal customers
3. Level 3: Taking Care Of those First-Time customers once you get them in there
4. Level 4: Inspiring Iron-Clad Loyalty
5. Level 5: Customers to start Referring Others back To You.

Customer Referral System

If you are running a good business then, getting referrals from your past customers can be a goldmine for you. However, you always want your customer referral program to be a win. Therefore, you reward the customer who's referring someone and you reward the referral for coming in to your business.

Motivate Your Customers To Refer More

There are dozens of ways to motivate your customers to refer more of their friends, family and social circle so here's what you do:

- You can host parties for local events or celebrations and offer free food to everyone who registers.
- You can host the fundraiser that benefits a local cause and require everyone to buy a raffle ticket and give you their contact information so that you can send them their prize.
- You may give your past customer loyalty rewards points for every first time customer they refer.
- You can give away prizes like iPhones, amazon gift cards or even vacations to customers who refer certain amounts of first-time customers to your business.

How To Build Your Business Referral Generating System (aka. Strategic Marketing Alliances)

When two businesses work together to create a joint marketing campaign that benefits or drives customer growth to both businesses, it's called a strategic marketing alliance. This can be done by mailing out letters of recommendations or endorsements to each other's customers and prospects. But, it can also be something as simple as handing out coupons or vouchers to their own customers which will then encourage the customer to visit the business of their strategic marketing partner. Regardless of the specific strategy used, the principle is that two different businesses are helping each other to become more successful.

The Bigfoot of Businesses

Strategic alliances are very effective ways of getting customers on a consistent basis, but this strategy does require you to step outside of your comfort zone in order to pull it off. That's why 99.9% of business owners don't even try to use this powerful business building strategy. However, don't dismiss it as being too hard, because it's so powerful that it can single-handedly transform your struggling business into a success. That's why it's one of the best ways for you to drive tons of your ideal customers to your business every day of the week.

Why Are Strategic Marketing Alliances So Powerful?

Strategic marketing alliances are one of the most powerful strategies you can get involved in because of seven reasons:

1. You will build a list of targeted customers and prospects that are most likely to dine at your business.

2. If done right, you will profit every time you form a strategic alliance while also building your list.

3. Your partnerships are a good way to build great relationships with other business owners in your community that will pay off for years to come.

4. There's little to no advertising or additional marketing expense to get these customers or customers to come into your business.

5. You can get access to a list of paying customers where someone else has already done the hard work.

6. It's easier to please these customers because you come highly recommended from a trusted source of theirs.

7. Using strategic alliances allows you to instantly position yourself as the best business because you're coming recommended from a trusted business.

The Strategic Alliance Mindset

When it comes to setting up strategic marketing alliances, you need to make sure that your motives are pure. You need to approach this from a win-win perspective and not come across desperate or sleazy. You need to authentically come across as someone who is genuinely adding value to your strategic marketing partner. If you are blowing smoke, people can tell. However, if you're thrilled and enthusiastic, it will show and can have a positive impact on your potential partnership that's why you need to come up with at least three to five things that partnering with you will help accomplish for your strategic marketing alliance partner in their business.

What To Look For In A Strategic Marketing Partner

- You need a business that has a quality product or service that's a good fit for your customers.
- You need someone who believes in and practices consistent marketing and basic business building principles.
- You need someone who is trustworthy and operates in full integrity with everything they do.
- You need a business that you can feel proud of being associated with don't ever risk your reputation.
- And you need a business partner who is willing to work, invest in and have a plan to make the alliance a success.

#1: Endorsed Marketing Campaigns

An endorsed marketing campaign is when your strategic marketing partner creates some type of marketing piece where they directly recommend your business to their client database. This could be a direct mail campaign consisting of letters or postcards promoting your business with a list. Your strategic partner could also choose to send out an email blast to their database. In most cases, you would have a special offer for the customers that your strategic partner refers to you so that they know that you have a strategic alliance with that business.

.

The Power of Endorsements

Endorsements are powerful, at its core, every strategic marketing alliance depends on the endorsement of its partners to be successful. For example, if your business partners with a wedding planner, then you need that wedding planner to speak good things about your business to their clients. Without the infamous "good word" being said about you, then your marketing alliance will fall flat and not work as planned.

That's why strategic alliances with good endorsements will always work better than any ad or marketing message that you send out to a list of people who don't know you. Lastly, that's why endorsement-based strategic marketing alliances are often the most effective alliances.

Are You A Risky Investment?

While endorsement-based marketing alliances are the most effective for your business, you must also acknowledge that they pose the most risk for your alliance partner as well. The best way to minimize this risk is to let your partner sample your business and service first and then clearly spell out what the irresistible offer for the alliance will be. Because if you screw up and drop the ball with the people your partner sends to you, then not only do you look bad, but the business that refers you also looks bad.

That's why it's always best to pay special attention to the customers that come to your business as a result of your alliance partnership. You may want to offer them special seating, parking or any number of special privileges so that the word will get back to your alliance partner that you treated them well.

In-Business Promotion Campaign

This promotion campaign is when you and your strategic partner create marketing materials to physically be or to be physically placed in both of your businesses to promote each other. This could be things like:

- Podium stands with tear-offs, images and advertising messages actively promoting your partner.
- Flyers placed in the business which advertise a coupon or voucher for customers.
- Banners that are placed in the business with an advertising message on the banner

Co-Marketing Campaign

A co-marketing campaign is an entire marketing campaign designed to promote the business of each strategic marketing partner. Things like Newspaper, television, radio and social media ads with both companies advertising complementary products and services. This requires two businesses that are very much related to each other and valuable to the customer. This option also requires a high level of trust and tends to be the most expensive and complex option, But, the rewards of this option can be worth the risk if you do it well.

So, Before You Say I Do

So before you say I do you must be able to provide a high level quality experience for the leads your alliance partner or your referrals are sending to you. You should be prepared to create a true win-win partnership where you both get something good out of the deal. You need you make sure you have best deals around compared to your competitors.

You need to have your systems in place to track the leads or sales the alliance generates. You also need to have your tracking systems being as simple as possible as the customer needing to bring a special coupon or know a specific word or phrase may visit your business you don't want it to be complicated,

Imagine

Imagine you find five strategic marketing partners lists that each have a list of 1,000 people. By partnering with them, you've now you've just become the business of choice for 5,000 quality referrals from other businesses…with NO extra advertising cost!

Word Of Caution…

On the other hand, the wrong strategic marketing alliance can do massive damage to your business's reputation. That's why you must have systems in place to consistently deliver good food and a good experience.

So, if you're not ready to handle the influx of customers, then don't do it. Also, you need to be prepared give more than you're getting to make the strategic alliance attractive. And you need to have several ideas a success for your alliance partner and your referrals.

All The Way To The Finish Line...

Even after you've set up a strategic marketing alliance, you need to stay on top of things to make sure you're partner doesn't drop the ball. You should find a reason to stop by, email or call them to update them and let them know you're available if they have any questions. You need to stay positive even if you're not seeing any results at first. Sometimes it takes a few weeks or even a few months for things to come together just right. Just be sure to get your partner to agree to a specific timeline for things to be completed to avoid any potential issues. If they start to lag, jump in and ask if there's anything you can do to help.

Why Good Partnerships Go Bad

When you find a good alliance partner, you need to protect that relationship like you would protect your gold.

When good strategic marketing go sour, it's usually because one or both of the partners are:

- Being cheap and not sharing costs evenly.
- Being inflexible about dates, offers and compensation.
- Being too casu.al about the partnership
- Making the other partner do too much work.
- Haven't built a good relationship or rapport with each other.
- Being desperate.
- Being greedy

CHAPTER 8

Follow-Up Marketing Systems:
How To Consistently Generate Massive Amounts of Leads, Sales And Profits From Your In-House Database

By now you already know that building your own in-house database of leads, prospects and past customers is critical. Now I want to teach you the most effective and profitable ways to follow up with your database of prospects and customers and get them to purchase from you time and time again.

Following up with your database or nurturing your leads consistently is your new philosophy that you must whole-heartedly adopt in your business to be successful. However, it's more than just sending sales messages.

Your goal is to own the space in your customers mind for the products and services that you sell. See the truth is prospects and customers always forget about your business over time. No matter how great the connection at the time a lead contacts or visits your business, the longer you wait to follow up with them, the more they forget you.

That's why your mission is to build relationships with qualified prospects regardless of their timing to buy, with the goal of earning their business when they are ready to buy. You accomplish this by consistently presenting the prospect with a persuasive sales message or educational message that compels them to visit your business and buy. You want them to feel as if they MUST come to ONLY your business when they're ready to buy AND when they're looking for information prior to buying.

Profitable Relationships

Follow-up marketing (also known as lead nurturing) is all about building a consensual relationship with a prospect — you can't force someone to commit (to a purchase, in this case) — but you also cannot afford to lose individuals because they're not ready to buy today.

Most leads will eventually be ready, but it is up to you to both provide them with relevant information and to be there when they are ready to make a buying decision. The truth is that up to 95 percent of qualified prospects that walk through your doors each day are there to research and are not yet ready to make a buying decision but as many as 70 percent of them will eventually buy a product or service from you — or your competitors.

The Ugly Truth

"Even a low quality product or service with lousy customer service can generate millions of dollars in sales with a consistent follow-up marketing plan it's been done time and time again."

Business Insurance

Building a list of past customers and prospects that you can market your business to "on-demand" is your insurance policy

Watch This **FREE** Video Now & Discover A New Era Of Internet Marketing:
www.AndrewCocks.ca

against the revenue roller coaster most business owners have to endure.

Your database should be filled with thousands of leads, prospects and past customers who you can email, call or mail an offer to any time that you choose. Imagine the power of sending out an email, text, postcard or letter on Tuesday and being booked solid or flooded with customers for the next two weeks from that one marketing effort. That's powerful.

However, the reality is that most business owners do the opposite. They spend thousands of dollars each month trying to get the attention of a small percentage of people who may possibly be ready to buy today, but do little to keep in contact with people who have already purchased from them and/or raised their hand in some way to say they're interested in what they're selling.

Don't Be An Average Joe

When it comes to follow up marketing, your goal is to not be an average business owner. Don't…spend thousands of dollars on advertising with newspaper, radio, television, postcards or letters, then sit back wish and hope the ad is good enough to attract new customers to cover the costs of ad and make a little profit. That's a tragedy that's replayed over and over in businesses all across the country.

Successful Business Owners Know That The Money Is In The List

The long-term and sustainable profits are in having a list of happy past customers and prospects to consistently market your offers to. If a person calls/walks-in/emails/visits your website or steps into your business...then you simply **MUST** make a conscious effort get their contact info. If you fail to do that you will likely lose that lead forever.

Most business owners:

- Look at ongoing marketing to their past customers and leads as a expense instead of an investment.
- They are not willing to take the time away from their business to create a multi-step campaign that runs consistently.
- Are so busy working in their business that they don't have time to work on their business and create systems that will generate a huge increase in profits.
- Don't know and refuse to learn how to write educational, entertaining and persuasive marketing sales messages.
- Get overwhelmed by the technology required to setup automated follow-up marketing systems.

Most Common Excuses

Unfortunately many business owners know the benefits of follow up marketing, but they allow themselves to buy into excuses that hold them back from getting the most lucrative type of customer back into their business.

The most common excuses are:

- Can't afford to pay for marketing to their database.
- Don't have their customers or prospect's information.
- Even if they had their contact information, don't know what to say.
- Don't know how to contact the customers or leads.
- Already have one million things going on right now.
- Don't have someone to do this for them.
- It seems too complicated.
- Don't want to learn to use any more technology.

Secrets To Follow-Up Marketing Success

In this section, I want to share with you the most powerful secrets that will allow you to experience massive success when you setup and implement your follow up marketing strategies.

Follow Up Marketing Success Secret #1:

The first follow up marketing success secret is to completely understand the buyers in your target market. You need to interview and survey your customers, as well as those that didn't buy from you, in order to define your ideal customer profile and develop buyer personas. You should ask questions like:

- What are their pains? What are their desires?
- What is their purchase process?
- Why were they interested in your product or service in the first place?
- What were the major factors in their purchasing decision?
- What else do you they want from your company?

Follow Up Marketing Success Secret #2:

The second follow up marketing success secret is pinpointing and knowing the buying stage cycles for your products and services. This is so important because in order to create a follow-up marketing and nurture campaign that works you must consistently deliver timely and relevant information to your prospects. If the information is too late, too soon or not relevant, it won't work.

You need to know and fully understand those stages and what works best with each. All buyers go through these three stages:

The Buying Stage Cycles

1. **Stage #1: Just Started Looking**

   a. To get these prospects to come and buy from you need to have things like: Free whitepapers, free books, free guides & tip sheets, free eBooks, free checklists, free videos, free kits and any combination of the above.

2. **Stage #2: Already Looking, But Need More Information**

   a. You need to offer things like free webinars & teleseminars, case studies, free product or service sample, frequently asked questions sheet requests, product spec sheets, catalogs etc.

3. **Stage #3: Ready To Buy Now**

   a. You want things like free trials, demos, free consultations, estimates or quotes, coupons.

Follow Up Marketing Success Secret #3

This success secret is all about analyzing your past marketing campaigns in order to determine how they contributed to revenue. You'll look at the percentage of responses to campaigns and determine how many leads moved through all stages, and the messages and content offered at each stage.

You should have a folder and binder (physical or on a computer) with every ad, promotion and sale you've ever run and the results of each. Otherwise how will you know what worked and how you can improve upon it? Reviewing the success (or failure) of your past marketing efforts is the foundation upon which you build your follow-up campaigns.

Follow Up Marketing Success Secret #4

This success secret is about visually mapping out the purchase path for each of your core products and services. You should have a piece of paper(s) where you've mapped out your follow up marketing campaigns that essentially mirrors your actual buying process.

The key to mapping this out is to start out with the end goal in mind and create a roadmap that is specifically designed to get a prospect to that end goal.

Be sure to develop a roadmap that makes the most sense for your business and try to anticipate any roadblocks to implementing it and address them early. If the objective is to send six emails and make three phone calls over eight weeks, what happens if you don't get the intended response after you do that? You need to have a plan for that.

Follow Up Marketing Success Secret #5

This follow up success secret is all about automating your entire follow-up campaigns as much as possible. You already have enough on your plate to worry about. You don't want to have to manually send every email, lick every envelope, print every postcard etc. Your follow-up campaigns must be able to be 99% automated with little human interaction needed to deploy or maintain the campaigns.

An automated "welcome campaign" is a great place to get started. Set up automated communications to greet those who enter your database and start delivering educational information right away.

There are over ten follow-up marketing campaigns you can and should implement in your business right away. Yes, setting up these campaigns sounds like a lot of work, although it really isn't, but the trade-off is HUGE for your profits bottom line.

Do the work once and profit from it for years.

11 Types of Follow-Up Marketing Campaigns

Follow-up Campaign #1: Promotional Offer

This type of follow-up campaign is used to generate an instant influx of sales and profits by making an irresistible offer to your database. The promotional offer follow-up campaign can be used for all contacts on your database list – non-buyers and past customers alike.

The most important part of this follow up campaign is that it must be built around an enticing and irresistible offer. It can't just be your normal every day and ordinary prices and packages that you always offer. You must also put an expiration date on the promotional offer so that people are forced to make a decision within the timeline you choose.

Follow-up Campaign #2: Post Purchase

This type of follow up campaign is designed for buyers only. The first couple of steps in this campaign should always revolve around:

1. Thanking the buyer for their purchase.
2. Reinforcing the good decision they made to purchase from you.
3. Share best practices to get the most out of their recent purchase.

After you've done those three key things, you can get very creative with the remainder of the campaign and do things like:

- Upsell closely related products or services.
- Cross-sell different types of other products or services that may complement their purchase.
- Deepen the relationship by continuing to educate the buyer on their purchase and share additional great features about their purchase.

Follow-up Campaign #3: Competitor Comparison

This type of follow-up campaign works great for companies that are in intensely competitive industries. This campaign focuses on educating your database on all the reasons why you're better than your competition. It can and should include case studies, testimonials and real-world test results from users of your product or services.

In order to be most effective, you could choose to have each message you send to your database focus on one key element of your product or service that is superior to your competition. However, make sure that you don't make personal attacks against your competitor. Focus on the superiority of your product or service only.

Follow-up Campaign #4: Top of Mind

This type of follow-up campaign is designed to keep your business in the forefront of a prospect or customers mind. This campaign can work well for any type of business, but it's a necessity for businesses that sell products or services with a longer life cycle like the real estate, mortgages, car industry etc.

While the goal of this campaign is not necessarily to sell a customer a product or service in every message, the occasional promotional message should be included. This campaign should be heavily branded with your logo, colors, unique sales proposition so that it's easily and instantly recognized as coming from your company.

Follow-up Campaign #5: Reengagement

This follow up campaign is all about getting past customers and prospects to interact with your company in some way. It could be through purchasing, but it should be through any number of ways like:

Watch This **FREE** Video Now & Discover A New Era Of Internet Marketing:
www.AndrewCocks.ca

- Requesting a catalog.
- Responding to an email.
- Calling into your office for more information.
- Visiting a website.
- Watching a video.

The reengagement campaign is all about getting past customers or prospects that showed interest previously to take another action to reconnect with your business in some way.

Follow-up Campaign #6: Renewal

This follow-up campaign is for customers who previously bought a series of products or ongoing service from you. The whole point of this campaign is to get them to once again signup for the service that they previously cancelled or that ran its course. It doesn't necessarily have to be a renewal of the service they've previously purchased. It can be a subscription to another service or series of products that you believe will help them. Just like when you're making a promotional offer, your success will be dependent on your ability to make an irresistible offer. If you primarily sell products without the option for ongoing services, now would be a great time to start offering subscriptions.

Follow-up Campaign #7: Topic-Based Campaign

This type of campaign is when you want to share information with your database on a specific topic. Of course the topics you share should be closely related to products or services that you sell so that the contact can consume the information and then go on to purchase from you.

This type of campaign is great for building and deepening your relationship with your database as well. Also, while the first few messages in this campaign may be educational only, the final few should directly point the contact to your product or service that fits with the messages you've been sending to them.

Follow-up Campaign #8: Upsell

This type of follow-up campaign is designed to sell the customer additional products and services that complement their original purchase.

The power of this campaign is that it instantly increases your sales and profits without a huge increase in advertising expense.

In your upsell follow up marketing campaign, you can offer:

- More of the same product or service they initially purchased.
- A larger quantity of the product or service they purchased.
- A bundle or package of additional services or products.
- Different products or services that you believe will help the buyer's things like that.

Follow-up Campaign #9: Onboarding

This campaign consists of follow up messages that help a new customer get up and running with the product or service they purchased from you.

This campaign is an absolute necessity when the product or service you sell is complicated and requires specific set of actions to maximize its benefits.

Many times you will see examples of onboarding follow up campaigns when a customer purchased technology dependent products or services. However, every business should have some form of onboarding to help their customers get the most value out of their purchase.

Follow-up Campaign #10: Training

This type of campaign allows you to focus on training your customers on the best way to use your products or services.

This campaign can also be a way for you to recommend additional products and services that will also help the customer. This training can be provided in the form of reports, books, videos, and webinars or in your business in a physical location.

You can also provide training on all the ways other customers are using your products and services.

And don't be shy about promoting your other products and services during your trainings. That has proven to be an effective way to increase sales in a non-salesy way.

Follow-up Campaign #11: Blend of All Campaign Types

What you've probably already noticed is that you probably could use several or more of the follow-up campaigns in your business running at the same time.

That's normal and to be expected. In fact, it's common to add all of the campaigns at some point. For example: A post-purchase campaign can lead into a onboarding campaign which can flow into a upsell campaign which goes into training campaign etc. However, it's virtually impossible to do that without using automation technology. So, in the next section I'm going to talk about automating your systems.

Creating a multi-channel follow-up marketing campaign that is affordable, produces high quality leads and runs on autopilot is the secret to practically all long-term successful companies. So I'm going to share with you the top six methods you can use to follow up with prospects leads or customers.

The Top Six Methods You Can Use To Follow Up With Prospects, Leads Or Customers

Follow-Up Method #1: Email

The first follow-up method is email. The majority of the country has email address that they check weekly and daily basis in most cases, so it makes complete business sense to use email to follow up with your past customers and prospects.

Also, if you have a website, then you can likely send out emails for free. The good news is that you can sit down once and write the emails and then they can be scheduled weeks and months in advance and can be recycled and used again. So once you do the initial work you don't have to repeat it again you just set it up.

Sending emails is a great way to build a relationship with your prospects and clients and its 100% trackable so you know who is opening and what's working. And best of all it's virtually free to send out an email free.

Follow-Up Method #2: Text Message.

The second follow up method is text message or sms. This method has the highest open rate of all marketing communications. It's similar to when email first came out. The good news is that it can be used to generate instant sales and profits because of the high open rate. Just like email, it's 100% trackable so you know who is opening and what's working. And it only costs one or two cents per text to send out.

Follow-Up Method #3: Recorded Message Voice Blasts

The third follow up method is by pre-recording a message by phone and sending it to your list. Most businesses don't try to make the human connection series, so your real message will stand out if you are using a voice blast. Plus, it creates a stronger bond to your customers when they hear your voice. You can set this up and have a campaign going within five to ten minutes and you can create your campaign online.

Follow-Up Method #4: Postcards

The fourth follow up method is sending postcards. Postcards are a simple, inexpensive, but effective way to send your marketing message. The receiver is practically guaranteed to see your marketing message when you send out a postcard.

The marketing message tends to be simpler and effective because the postcard is limited in size and it's really affordable to at 50+ cents per postcard.

Follow-Up Method #5: Letters/Newsletters or Sales letters

The fifth follow up method is sending a newsletter or sales letter. Your newsletter or sales letter can range in length from one page to ten pages or more. The extra length allows you tell your story in a compelling and persuasive way while generating sales. It also allows your customers to see behind the curtain of your business and see that you're just like..

Follow-Up Method #6: Live Phone Calls

The sixth follow up method is a live phone call. This can be a customer service follow up call/survey to see what other products and services your customers want from you.

People are desperate to know businesses care about their input and feedback. So, giving them a customer service or survey call makes them feel good. It's very affordable to do because you already have phone lines in your office. And it's easy and simple to actually implement as it's just a phone call.

The Best Part Is...

- Five of these six follow-up marketing strategies can be automated and scheduled months in advance.
- More importantly, because they're automated and require very little human intervention, there's little chance for error.

- So few businesses are doing this, that you will stand heads and shoulders above your competition in your marketplace.
- Plus, more importantly you will have a proven marketing plan to generate sales consistently.
- And the R.O.I. is HUGE. In many cases you're spending less than $100 with the potential to generate tens of thousands of dollars in sales month after month.

Watch This **FREE** Video Now & Discover A New Era Of Internet Marketing:
www.AndrewCocks.ca

CHAPTER 9

Profit Maximization Systems:
How To Consistently Generate More
Sales And Profits Without Spending
More Money On Advertising

E very business owner knows that he needs a consistent flow of new customers in order to keep sales rolling in. However, the same business owner probably doesn't realize that he can increase sales and profits by upwards of thirty percent or more by getting existing customers to purchase more.

The process, systems or strategies to get customers to purchase more is called profit maximization. Your profit maximization systems could be anything and everything you do to get customers to purchase more from you after their initial purchase.

What Makes Profit Maximization Systems So Important?

What makes profit maximization systems so important is that they can single-handedly transform a loss leader into a front-end lead generation system that generates consistent profits.

A properly implemented profit maximization system will stabilize your revenue and sales and allow you to forecast more accurately. When you know that every customer or lead you generate is worth much more than their initial purchase, it gives you peace of mind to invest more in your business.

Profit Maximization Systems Are Flexible

The best thing about profit maximization systems is that they are flexible and can be completely customized to fit perfectly with your business. You can create your profit maximization systems products or services personally and expand your own brand. You can also use other businesses products or services as your profit maximization systems by working together with them or becoming a distributor for those other companies.

Also if you have a good CRM system, you can even create a custom profit maximization system for each individual customer or you can use a general profit maximization systems sales funnel for all customers.

The 3 Ways To Grow Your Business

All strategies, tools and techniques that you could use to maximize your profits fall into one of three categories:

1. Get more customers.
2. Get existing customers to buy more frequently.
3. Sell more stuff to your existing customers.

Most businesses owners feel like their job is done once the initial sale is made, but nothing can be further from the truth. As a business owner, the real work has only just begun.

The real profits are in all the additional products and services you can sell that same customer after they make their initial purchase. All the products or services you sell your customer after their initial purchase, can be called your profit maximization strategies.

Three Main Profit Maximization Strategies

There are three main profit maximization strategies that you need to implement in your business. They are:

1. **Upsell Strategy** - Upsell simply means selling your customer something of higher value or an additional product or service at the time of purchase.
2. **Downsell Strategy** - Downsells are when you sell a scaled-down or feature-lite version of a product or service to a customer who didn't purchase your original offer.. Usually downsells are cheaper in price than the original or upsell.

3. **Cross-Sell Strategy** - Cross-selling is when you sell a current customer something else that may or may not be related to their original purchase. This can happen at the time of purchase, but it usually happens after the initial purchase and closely related upsell.

Building Your Profit Maximization Systems

You may not realize this, but the profit maximization systems of your business have the potential to produce much more profit than the initial purchase your customer makes with you.

Your mindset should be that if a customer trusted your business enough to make the initial purchase, then your belief must be that with a proper follow up campaign, they will buy other products or services from you.

A well-developed profit maximization system can transform a mediocre business into a super-successful business. You should focus on building your profit maximization systems as quickly as possible in order to capture the money that you're now leaving on the table.

The Magic Of The Profit Maximization Systems

Your profit maximization systems should consist of upsells, down-sells, cross-sells and conversion improvement strategies. If your profit maximization systems is well thought out and implemented properly, you can even afford to take a loss on the front-end service or product just to get customers into your funnel. You can even choose to spend more to get that front-end customer because you know the numbers and value of each customer.

When I say profit maximization systems, I'm talking about anything you can do to increase your profits after the first time transaction including:

- One time sales
- Products added to services
- Services added to products
- More services that you sell them
- More products that you sell them
- Recurring sales

Never Stop Building

No matter how good you feel your business systems are right now, you should never stop adding to your profit maximization systems. As long as you are in business you should be brainstorming, repackaging, inventing, renaming, bundling products and services that can be introduced and then reintroduced to your new customers.

Also if you're strategic and invest a little more time at the beginning to plan out your profit maximization systems path, the day will come where you have months or even years of campaigns created. When you have all your profit maximization systems offers and promotional material and systems setup, you could literally walk away from your business for months at a time and your profits will still flow in.

The Profit Maximization Systems Difference

Let's walk through an example to illustrate the power of a well thought out profit maximization.

1. Business owner A sells 1000 widgets at $50 to each new customer and earns $50,000 per month from the sales.

2. Business owner B sells 1,000 widgets at $50 to each new customer, but because he has well-planned profit maximization systems, he's able to get 30% of his past customers to purchase an additional two items generating an additional $125 per customer per month.

3. Both business owners generated the $50,000 on the front-end but only business owner #2 generates an additional $37,500 in sales each month due to his profit maximization systems.

It's Obvious...Isn't It?

In other words they don't have profit maximization systems in place. However, the vast majority of business owners do next to nothing to make it happen. The longer a customer is purchasing from you, the more profitable and valuable that customer becomes to your business. Selling to your customers more frequently allows you to extend the lifetime value of your customers.

When you create strategies to sell to your customers more frequently, you also have a much better chance of getting those customers back who may have disconnected from your business. Also when you combine upsells and cross-sells with your customers buying more frequently you can see phenomenal increases in revenue and profits.

The 7 Key Factors That Influence Customer Buying Frequency

Key Factor #1 - High Value Products And Services

Many times business owners try to give the customers what they (the business owner) *think* is valuable. You must get feedback from your customers in order to decide what they perceive as being valuable. It's not about you...it's about them. You must always focus on consistently providing high value from the customer's perspective. Use the input your customers give you, but you'll most likely find that perceived value is a combination of customer satisfaction and intelligent pricing.

Key Factor #2 – Unique Offers

Unique and compelling offers are very powerful because the customer begins to feel that you are a market leader. Your customers must view you as always being relevant otherwise you become irrelevant and that's when you begin to have a huge drop-off in your marketing efforts.

By developing unique and compelling offers, you subconsciously communicate to your customers that you are invested in helping them achieve their desired results and outcomes. The only way to develop unique and compelling offers is by tuning in to your customer's wants, needs, goals and desires. The process of collecting this information improves your ability to create more effective marketing campaigns.

Key Factor #3 - Make Them Feel Special

Everyone wants to feel cared for and connected to something meaningful. Your customers are no exception to that. You must show them that they matter to you and that they're more than just a number or dollar sign. Your customers are the focal point of your business; you should let them know that they are special and important to you.

Your goal is to show your customers you care and help them develop a special connection to you and your business that they simply can't get anywhere else.

Key Factor #4 - Constant Communication

If you don't communicate with your customers on a regular basis, you are slowly but surely being forgotten. Your ability to increase the purchase frequency of your customers is directly tied to your consistency in communicating with them. If you want your customers to buy from you for as long as you're in business, you need to communicate with them for as long as you're in business. But it's more than just marketing. You're nurturing your leads in a well-rounded way that doesn't scream sell, sell, sell.

Key Factor #5 - Pricing Incentives

One of the most powerful, but often abused frequency strategies is discounting and pricing incentives. You don't always have to discount your prices to incentivize your customers to buy more from you. In fact, if at all possible, you'll want to do everything in your power to avoid discounting your prices in order to increase frequency.

Try working towards getting the customers to buy bigger quantities or bundles of packages which allow you to train your customers to not expect a discount. Essentially, the formula is to reward your customers for buying more often at higher profit margins. That's a recipe for success.

Key Factor #6 -Various Longevity Bonuses

You can reward your customers based on how long they've been buying from you. It's good because you're training your customers to be loyal. This is a great strategy because it promotes and encourages your customers to actively purchase from you. You can surprise your customers with the bonuses or you can let them know upfront what they can receive in exchange for being loyal and active. Using this strategy keeps your focus off of discounting your prices and fees in order to incentivize your customers to purchase more often.

Key Factor #7 - Product Or Service Upgrades

You should always create a clear path for customers to step up your product or service ladder. If you can't come up with a path, then I guarantee that your customers don't know the path and you're losing out on revenues and profits. Your upgrades can be based on features or quantity. Regardless of the upgrade path you choose, it should always include an increase in price to justify the step up.

The Bottom Line

There are dozens of marketing campaigns and systems you can and should implement in your business right away. Yes, setting up these campaigns and systems is a lot of work initially but the trade-off is HUGE for your profits bottom line. Do the work once and profit from it for years.

www.ingramcontent.com/pod-product-compliance
Lightning Source LLC
Chambersburg PA
CBHW051323170526
45166CB00002B/666